D1317921

Daniel

Detail from the ceiling of the Sistine Chapel in Rome, painted by Michelangelo, showing the prophet Daniel recording his visions.

Money at its Best:
Millionaires of the Bible

MONEY
at its
BEST

Daniel

Cheryl A. Paden

Mason Crest Publishers
Philadelphia

Produced by OTTN Publishing.
Cover design © 2009 TLC Graphics, www.TLCGraphics.com.

Mason Crest Publishers
370 Reed Road, Suite 302
Broomall PA 19008
www.masoncrest.com   DEC 2 2 2009

First printing

1 3 5 7 9 8 6 4 2

Library of Congress Cataloging-in-Publication Data

   Paden, Cheryl A.
    Daniel / Cheryl A. Paden
       p. cm. — (Money at its best: millionaires of the Old
   Testament)
    Includes bibliographical references.
    ISBN 978-1-4222-0467-2 (hardcover)
    ISBN 978-1-4222-0842-7 (pbk.)
    1. Daniel (Biblical figure)—Juvenile literature. 2. Bible. O.T.—
   Biography—Juvenile literature. I. Title.
    BS580.D2 P33 2008
    224/.5092—dc22

                                    2008020869

Publisher's Note: The Web sites listed in this book were active at the time of
publication. The publisher is not responsible for Web sites that have changed their
address or discontinued operation since the date of publication. The publisher reviews
and updates the Web sites each time the book is reprinted.

Table of Contents

Daniel and His Wealth

● Daniel was born into a noble family in the kingdom of Judah; however, while he was still a teenager, his homeland was overthrown, and he was taken into Babylonian captivity. His misfortunes quickly changed when King Nebuchadnezzar ordered his court official "to bring in some of the Israelites from the royal family and the nobility—young men without any physical defect, handsome, showing aptitude for every kind of learning, well informed, quick to understand, and qualified to serve in the king's palace" (Daniel 1:3-4).

● Daniel and his friends Shadrach, Meshach, and Abednego impressed the king more than all the other young men. "To these four young men God gave knowledge and understanding of all kinds of literature and learning. And Daniel could understand visions and dreams of all kinds" (Daniel 1:17). As members of the king's household, they were given every luxury. Daniel was wealthy again, thanks to his staunch belief that God would take care of him.

● King Nebuchadnezzar had a nightmare one night that none of his astrologers could interpret. Daniel asked for the answer through prayer, and God revealed the meaning of the dream to Daniel. Nebuchadnezzar increased Daniel's wealth substantially because he was able to help the king.

● Daniel also served under King Darius, the Persian king whose armies conquered Babylon. The king trusted Daniel, making him one of the highest-ranking officials in the kingdom.

● Daniel was betrayed by the other court officials for not worshipping King Darius, and was thrown into the lions' den. His wealth and life were in jeopardy, but he believed God would save him from a wrongful death. The next morning, he said to the king: "My God sent his angel, and he shut the mouths of the lions. They have not hurt me, because I was found innocent in his sight. Nor have I ever done any wrong before you, O king" (Daniel 6:22).

● Daniel prospered because God blessed him. Daniel walked with God, and time and again his faith saved his life. Each time he overcame a challenge, he acknowledged God's help and grace, and in turn, God protected him and elevated him to positions of prestige and honor. Daniel possessed great material wealth, but his true treasure was his absolute faith in God.

INTRODUCTION: WEALTH AND FAITH

Many people believe strongly that great personal wealth is incompatible with deep religious belief—that like oil and water, the two cannot be mixed. Christians, in particular, often feel this way, recollecting Jesus Christ's own teachings on wealth. "Do not store up for yourselves treasures on earth, where moth and rust destroy, and where thieves break in and steal," Jesus cautions during the Sermon on the Mount (Matthew 6:19). In Luke 18:25, he declares, "It is easier for a camel to go through the eye of a needle than for a rich man to enter the kingdom of God"—a sentiment repeated elsewhere in the Gospels.

Yet in Judeo-Christian culture there is a long-standing tradition of material wealth as the manifestation of God's blessing. This tradition is amply reflected in the books of the Hebrew Bible (or as Christians know them, the Old Testament). Genesis 13:2 says that the patriarch Abram (Abraham) "had become very wealthy in livestock and in silver and gold"; the Bible makes it clear that this prosperity is a gift from God. Other figures whose lives are chronicled in

7

Genesis—including Isaac, Jacob, Joseph, Noah, and Job—are described as both wealthy and righteous. The book of Deuteronomy expresses God's promise of prosperity for those who obey his commandments:

> If you fully obey the Lord your God and carefully follow all his commands I give you today, the Lord your God will set you high above all the nations on earth. . . . The Lord will grant you abundant prosperity—in the fruit of your womb, the young of your livestock and the crops of your ground—in the land he swore to your forefathers to give you. (Deuteronomy 28:1, 11)

A key requirement for this prosperity, however, is that God's blessings must be used to help others. Deuteronomy 15:10–11 says, "Give generously . . . and do so without a grudging heart; then because of this the Lord your God will bless you in all your work and in everything you put your hand to." The book of Proverbs—written during the time of Solomon, one of history's wealthiest rulers—similarly presents wealth as a desirable blessing that can be obtained through hard work, wisdom, and following God's laws. Proverbs 14:31 promises, "The faithless will be fully repaid for their ways, and the good man rewarded for his."

Numerous stories and folktales show the generosity of the patriarchs. According to Jewish legend, Job owned an inn at a crossroads, where he allowed travelers to eat and drink at no cost. When they offered to pay, he instead told them about God, explaining that he was simply a steward of the wealth that God had given to him and urging them to worship God, obey God's commands, and receive their own blessings. A story about Abraham says that when he moved his flocks from one field to another, he would muzzle the animals so that they would not graze on a neighbor's property.

After the death of Solomon, however, the kingdom of Israel

was divided and the people fell away from the commandments God had mandated. The later writings of the prophets, who are attempting to correct misbehavior, specifically address unethical acts committed to gain wealth. "You trample on the poor," complained the prophet Amos. "You oppress the righteous and take bribes and you deprive the poor of justice in the courts" (Amos 5:11, 12). The prophet Isaiah insists, "Learn to do right! Seek justice, encourage the oppressed. . . . If you are willing and obedient, you will eat the best from the land; but if you resist and rebel, you will be devoured by the sword" (Isaiah 1:17, 19–20).

Viewed in this light, the teachings of Jesus take on new meaning. Jesus does not condemn wealth; he condemns those who would allow the pursuit of wealth to come ahead of the proper relationship with God: "No one can serve two masters. . . . You cannot serve both God and money" (Matthew 6:24).

Today, nearly everyone living in the Western world could be considered materially wealthier than the people of the Bible, who had no running water or electricity, lived in tents, walked when traveling long distances, and wore clothing handmade from animal skins. But we also live in an age when tabloid newspapers and trashy television programs avidly follow the misadventures of spoiled and selfish millionaire athletes and entertainers. In the mainstream news outlets, it is common to read or hear reports of corporate greed and malfeasance, or of corrupt politicians enriching themselves at the expense of their constituents. Often, the responsibility of the wealthy to those members of the community who are not as successful seems to have been forgotten.

The purpose of the series MONEY AT ITS BEST: MILLIONAIRES OF THE BIBLE is to examine the lives of key figures from biblical history, showing how these people used their wealth or their powerful and privileged positions in order to make a difference in the lives of others.

This 11th-century mosaic from an Orthodox church in Greece depicts Daniel in the lion's den. His outstretched arms are meant to prefigure the sacrifice of Jesus on the cross.

HOPE FOR HIS PEOPLE

Daniel is one of the most familiar figures of Biblical history. As a teenager living in the country of Judah, Daniel was taken captive by a Babylonian king named Nebuchadnezzar, then the most powerful man in the world. But God blesses Daniel with a special talent, the ability to understand and interpret dreams and visions. His life is spared several times, thanks to this prophetic gift. What's more, this insight allows Daniel to look beyond his immediate situation and foretell a better day for himself and the Hebrew people, as well as to describe future events—including the end of the world!

Daniel's story is found in the Hebrew Bible, the ancient Jewish scriptures that roughly correspond to what Christians call the Old Testament. The book of Daniel is one of triumph under the worst of circumstances. As a member of a captive community in a foreign nation, Daniel exhibits moral excellence despite many hardships. His life serves as an example to people across time, cultures, and continents that we all have the capacity to emerge heroic—if, as related in the Book of Daniel, we exercise moral faith, spiritual courage, and, most importantly, an unwavering belief in God.

The Book of Daniel further makes clear that God reaches out to those who are ungodly and prideful because of their wealth and influence. With repentance and conversion, even they can find favor with God.

DANIEL IN POPULAR CULTURE

Often, children first learn about Daniel through the story about his experiences in the lion's den. Young children are often given crayons and instructed to color pictures of Daniel surrounded by lions. Eventually, children advance to the story of Daniel and his three friends Shadrach, Meshach, and Abednego. Nebuchadnezzar casts all of them into a blazing furnace, because they won't worship a colossal golden statute that he has put up. Yet, they survive; God saves them.

Even those who do not know anything about the Biblical Daniel will probably recognize two idioms that come straight from the book that bears his name: The popular expression "to see the handwriting on the wall" is used to indicate that someone knows something bad is going to happen. It refers to a story from the book of Daniel in which the king of Babylon saw a hand without a body write a mysterious message on a palace wall: "Mene, mene, tekel, parsin." None of the king's aides could interpret the message, so Daniel was sent to explain the meaning of the strange words. When he arrived, he told the king that it was a warning that his kingdom would be conquered. That night, this prophecy came true. Another expression used today, "to walk into the lion's den," is a warning that you're about to find yourself in a difficult situation or among enemies. This expression also comes from the book of Daniel, when the young man is thrown into a pit filled with lions.

Daniel is also memorialized in song. The refrain of a spiritual asks a simple yet profound question:

> Didn't my Lord deliver Daniel,
> Deliver Daniel, deliver Daniel,
> Didn't my Lord deliver Daniel
> An' why not every man.
>
> He delivered Daniel f'om de lion's den,
> Jonah f'om de belly of de whale,
> An' de Hebrew children f'om de fiery furnace
> An' why not every man?

HISTORICAL FACT OR FICTION

Though Daniel is one of the best-known figures of the Bible, he also is perhaps one of the least understood. The Book of Daniel is not easy to understand. There are questions about dates within Daniel and even its authorship. Then there's the fact that the book is written in two languages. The Book of Daniel begins in Hebrew, but changes to Aramaic at Chapter 2:4. The Aramaic continues to the end of Chapter 7, but the last five chapters are all written once again in Hebrew. To date, Biblical scholars have not found an explanation for the shift in language.

Scholarly debates also pivot on whether Daniel is a real historical figure, or a character in a folktale who was passed down through oral history to the Jewish people as a way to uplift them while they were captives in Babylon. In the Bible, the first half of this book, Chapters 1–6, contains stories written in the third person, while the second

The oldest versions of the book of Daniel known to exist today were part of the collection of ancient writings known as the Dead Sea Scrolls. (This is a fragment of a scroll from this collection.) The first of these scrolls were discovered by accident in 1947 in a cave at Qumran near Israel's Dead Sea. A shepherd was tossing stones into a cave, looking for a lost goat, when he heard a rock shatter something. Investigating further, the shepherd found that the rock had struck a clay container, causing it to break, and revealing seven scrolls. Over the next decade, archaeologists investigated ten other caves, where they discovered thousands of scroll fragments. All of them had survived for nearly 2,000 years, rolled up and placed in simple stone jars with lids. When compared to modern translations, scholars found that the Dead Sea texts were virtually identical to the Biblical books used by Christians and Jews today. This indicated that the Biblical writings have not been changed and edited over the last two millenia.

half is mostly told from first-person perspective. What's more, in the version of the Old Testament used by Roman Catholic and Eastern Orthodox churches, the book contains literature not found in versions of the Bible used by other Christians. These sections of Daniel are called the Prayer of Azariah, the Song of the Three Young Men, Susanna, and Bel and the Dragon.

There are even differences of opinion as to whether Daniel is a prophet. In the Jewish Talmud, Daniel is not recognized as a prophet, because according to Jewish tradition, he was not sent to the people of Israel with any prophecy. Instead, Talmudic and rabbinic literature considers him a saint, or an example. The Jewish tradition further maintains that Daniel's visions of the future were meant to be written down; as such, they are writings, not prophecies.

Christians, on the other hand, list Daniel as a major prophet—God allowed Daniel to interpret dreams and visions, and later he becomes the recipient of visions, which require interpretation by others.

Then there is Chapter Five in the Book of Daniel, which contains additional features that some find problematic. It is here that we learn about the mysterious disembodied hand that writes on a palace wall. Some argue that surely this could not have actually happened, which fuels the debate over whether the Book of Daniel is historical fact or fiction.

Whatever the truth about Daniel may never be resolved; such debates will no doubt continue. But it can be said that the Book of Daniel offers a message of hope and encouragement for captured, oppressed, and demoralized people, provides a model for how believers should conduct themselves, even in nations where God is not acknowledged as the one true God, and further, it illustrates that loyal obedience to God can be rewarded by worldly success.

A VISION FOR THE FUTURE

For thousands of years, people have been intrigued and worried about what the future holds for mankind. Hollywood movies and television shows are replete with examples of programs about people who can predict the future, or about the end of the world. The book industry is no different. One of the most popular book series of recent times has been the LEFT BEHIND series, which has as its theme the end times. This series of fictional novels has sold some 50 million copies, making it the best-selling Christian fiction series in history. Today, the series includes sixteen titles in the adult series, audio books, DVDs, and more. "In terms of its impact on Christianity, it's probably greater than that of any other book in modern times, outside the Bible," the late Christian fundamentalist Jerry Falwell said about *Left Behind: A Novel of the Earth's Last Days* (1995), during an interview with *Time* magazine.

But this type of literature is nothing new. The Book of Daniel, written more than 2,200 years ago, records four of Daniel's visions. These deal with the future, including a description of how the world will end. Daniel is one of several Biblical books that have inspired the writers of current books and films on this subject.

Daniel is considered a form of apocalyptic literature—a religious writing that records revelations from God by way of angels, dreams, and visions. Our English words apocalyptic and apocalypse come from a Greek word, *apokálypsis*, which means "to uncover" or "to reveal." Besides the Book of Daniel, another book in the Christian Bible stands as an example of this type of literature. That is the Revelation of John in the New Testament. In addition, passages of other books in the Bible are considered apocalyptic.

A feature of apocalyptic writings is encoded or symbolic language. For example, in Daniel, wild beasts represent the Gentile (or non-Jewish) nations, and animal horns represent Gentile rulers. One of the reasons that ancient

Mosaic decoration in a Greek Orthodox church on the island of Patmos depicts John, the author of the Biblical Book of Revelation. This book of the New Testament includes John's visions of the future and the end of the world. Revelation and Daniel are considered examples of apocalyptic literature. The Greek word apokálypsis *refers to an unfolding of things not previously known and which could not be known if they were not revealed by a greater power.*

writers used such language was to hide messages from enemies. Someone like Daniel could have used apocalyptic writing to hide messages from his captors, while revealing information to his fellow Jews.

"The Book of Daniel is the jewel of prophetical literature," writes author Les Brittingham in his book *Decoding Daniel: An In-Depth Study of the Book of Daniel.* He further states that "Daniel is perhaps the greatest of the Old Testament prophets in terms of scope and magnitude of impact."

CATASTROPHE AND CAPTIVITY

The book of Daniel begins by describing how Babylonian armies conquered Jerusalem—an event that occurred around the year 600 B.C.E. "In the third year of the reign of Jehoiakim king of Judah, Nebuchadnezzar king of Babylon came to Jerusalem and besieged it. And the Lord delivered Jehoiakim king of Judah into his hand, along with some of the articles from the temple of God. These he carried off to the temple of his god in Babylonia and put in the treasure house of his god" (Daniel 1:1–2).

To understand why God would allow the Babylonian king to attack and defeat his chosen people requires some historical background. In this sense, the story of Daniel begins with his ancestor Abraham, a man who is believed to have lived about 1,500 years before Daniel was born—approximately 4,000 years ago.

18

HISTORY OF THE ISRAELITES

Daniel's ancestor Abraham was born and raised in Ur of the Chaldees, a city in southern Mesopotamia. Ur was a center of idol worship and astrology. Abraham's father sold idols, but Abraham didn't believe in idols. He believed there was only one God. So God told Abraham to leave his father's home and country, and go to an unknown land known as Canaan. Abraham obeyed, taking along with him his wife Sarah, his nephew Lot, and others who believed, as he did, in one supreme God.

God, in turn, made a special pact, or covenant, with Abraham. In exchange for being faithful to His commands, God gave Abraham great riches, including land, silver and gold, herds of livestock, and protection from his enemies. God renewed the covenant with Abraham's younger son, Isaac, and with Abraham's grandson, Jacob.

Daniel was descended from Abraham, a man whom God promised would become the father of many nations. Abraham obeyed God, even when He demanded that Abraham sacrifice his son Isaac. Because of Abraham's faith and his willingness to follow God's commands, God permitted Abraham to sacrifice a ram in Isaac's place.

These men became known as the patriarchs, the ancestors of the Hebrew people. Because God gave Jacob the name Israel, the Hebrews—who were direct descendants of his twelve sons—were also called the Israelites.

According to the Bible, the Hebrews endured more than 400 years of slavery in Egypt before being led to freedom by Moses. God directed Moses to lead the Israelites to Mount Sinai, where he handed down the Ten Commandments, as well as hundreds of other laws and requirements that the Israelites were expected to follow. These laws are recorded in the Torah, the first five books of the Hebrew Bible. (The Hebrew Bible roughly corresponds to the Old Testament used by Christians; the Jewish laws given to Moses are primarily contained in the

Moses received the Ten Commandments while leading the Israelites out of captivity in Egypt to the land that God had promised them. That land is referred to as the Promised Land, or Canaan, and later it became the country of Israel. The Ten Commandments were laws written on stone tablets and given to the people of Israel. The Ten Commandments are found in the Book of Exodus, Chapter 20:3–17.

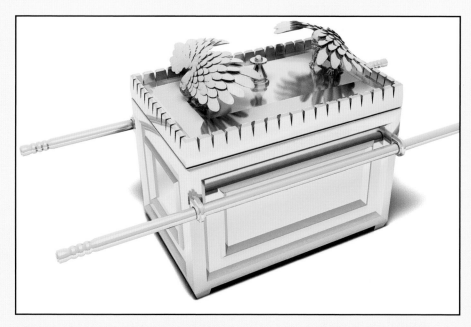

The Commandments were kept in a special chest called the Ark of the Covenant. The Ark of the Covenant, or sacred chest, was made of acacia wood and overlaid with pure gold and had a lid made of gold. The Hebrew people carried the ark as they traveled in the desert, waiting to enter the Promised Land. It was permanently lost during the Babylonian invasion, though reports that it has been found occasionally surface on news reports today.

books known to Christians as Exodus, Leviticus, and Deuteronomy.) Moses then led the Israelites back to Canaan, which God had promised that his people would inherit.

The dating of the Hebrews' time in Egypt and their subsequent wandering in the wilderness is uncertain. Most scholars believe that the Hebrews arrived at Canaan around 1200 B.C.E. and spent several centuries in periodic warfare with the people already living there, known as the Canaanites. Archaeological evidence indicates that around the year 1000 B.C.E., the Israelites were strong enough to conquer Canaan and establish their own kingdom, Israel.

During the reign of King David and his son, Solomon, Israel was a wealthy and powerful country. However, as time passed the descendants of Abraham started to turn their backs on the very God who had ensured their prosperity. Often, the kings of Israel led the way into wickedness. For example, even though King Solomon built a majestic temple in Jerusalem dedicated to the worship of the one God, later in his reign he strayed into idolatry.

After Solomon died, his sons and generals fought for the throne. A bloody civil war ensued, as God split the rebellious kingdom in two. Residents of the ten northern tribes followed Jeroboam, one of Solomon's generals, and formed the kingdom of Israel. The two southern tribes, Judah and Benjamin, remained loyal to Solomon's son Rehoboam. Their territory became the kingdom of Judah, with Jerusalem as its capital.

In the centuries that followed, both kingdoms became more distant from God, despite the efforts of many prophets to warn the people against their ungodly, violent, and wicked ways. Ultimately, the kingdom of Israel became so corrupted that it was destroyed. In 722 B.C.E., an Assyrian army commanded by Sargon II conquered the kingdom and led the Israelites away to slavery.

JUDAH UNDER SIEGE

Even after the Assyrians destroyed Judah, God continued to send prophets to warn the people of Judah to turn from their immoral and unjust ways. One of those prophets was Habakkuk, who lived in Judah and observed firsthand the injustice and cruelty of Israelite society. His writings record Habakkuk's complaints: "Our Lord, how long must I beg for your help before you listen? How long before you save us from all this violence? Why do you make me watch such terrible injustice? Why do you allow violence, law-

This model shows the central part of the temple to Yahweh that Solomon ordered to be built in Jerusalem. However, during his reign Solomon also constructed places where other gods could be worshipped. As a result, after Solomon's death the kingdom was divided into two states, Israel and Judah.

lessness, crime, and cruelty to spread everywhere?" (Habakkuk 1:2, 3)

God answers, but his response is not what the prophet expected to hear:

> Look at the nations and watch—
> And be utterly amazed.
> For I am going to do something in your days
> That you would not believe,
> Even if you were told.
>
> I am raising up the Babylonians,
> That ruthless and impetuous people,
> Who sweep across the whole earth
> To seize dwelling places not their own.
> They are a feared and dreaded people;
> They are a law to themselves
> And promise their own honor. (Habakkuk 1:5–7)

The Bible does not say when Habakkuk lived, but most scholars believe that he was active as a preacher in Judah around the year 612 B.C.E. Things would get worse, not better, in the next few years.

The narrative now returns to Jehoiakim, who is the first person named in the Book of Daniel. Jehoiakim was one of the worst kings to reign over Judah. He was the son of a godly king, Josiah, but Jehoiakim didn't follow in his

Though Habakkuk lived centuries ago, his question is still relevant today. It's almost inevitable that people will ask some version of this question at some point during their lives, which is to say, "Why do bad things happen to good people?"

father's footsteps. He was dishonest, and oppressive, and he reintroduced idolatrous worship in the temple during the years he ruled (from 611 to 600 B.C.E.). So God allowed the Babylonian king Nabopolassar (also known as Nebuchadnezzar I) with an army of men drawn from western Africa, Libya, and Ethiopia, to capture the city of Jerusalem. Nabopolassar was elderly and sick, however, so

Kings Who Ruled Judah

Rehoboam ruled seventeen years
(1 Kings 14:21)

Abijam ruled three years
(1 Kings 15:2)

Asa ruled forty-one years
(1 Kings 15:10

Jehoshaphat ruled twenty-five
years (1 Kings 22:42)

Jehoram ruled eight years
(2 Kings 8:17)

Ahaziah ruled part of one year
(2 Kings 8:25, 26)

Queen Athaliah ruled six years
(2 Kings 11:3)

Jehoash ruled forty years
(2 Kings 12:1)

Amaziah ruled twenty-nine years
(2 Kings 14:2)

Uzziah (also known as Azariah)
ruled fifty-two years
(2 Kings 15:2)

Jotham ruled sixteen years
(2 Kings 15:33)

Ahaz ruled sixteen years
(2 Kings 16:2)

Hezekiah ruled twenty-nine years
(2 Kings 18:1, 2)

Manasseh ruled fifty-five years
(2 Kings 21:1)

Amon ruled two years
(2 Kings 21: 19)

Josiah ruled thirty-one years
(2 Kings 22:1)

Jehoahaz ruled three months
(2 Kings 23: 31)

Jehoiakim ruled eleven years
(2 Kings 23:36)

Jehoiachin ruled three months
(2 Kings 24:8)

Zedekiah ruled eleven years
(2 Kings 24:18)

he appointed his son Nebuchadnezzar, the crown prince, commander in chief.

Nebuchadnezzar allowed Jehoiakim to rule as his puppet, or vassal king, in Jerusalem for three years, because he had received word of the sudden death of his father. Nebuchadnezzar immediately headed home to Babylon, crossing six-hundred miles of desert in two weeks. But he didn't leave empty-handed. As booty, he took treasures from the temple built by Solomon, and carried back with him to Babylon several key Hebrew nobles, including Daniel and his three friends. What happened to Jehoiakim is not clear. The Bible only records that he "rested with his fathers" (2 Kings 24:6).

Next came Jehoiachin, Jehoiakim's son. He ruled for only three months, and in that short time, "He did evil in the eyes of the Lord, just as his father had done" (2 Kings 24:9).

Jehoiachin rebelled, and in March 597 B.C.E, Nebuchadnezzar attacked Jerusalem again, sending in Babylonian troops to stop the unrest. This time around Nebuchadnezzar took Jehoiachin captive to Babylon, along with his mother, his wives, his high-ranking officials and leading men, his 7,000-strong army, and one thousand artisans. Then he made Mattaniah, Jehoiachin's uncle, king; he also changed the uncle's name to Zedekiah.

Jehoiachin and his family were kept in Babylon after the Babylonian raid on Jerusalem in 597 B.C.E. Clay ration receipts bearing the king's name have been found by archaeologists working in Babylon, confirming this piece of Biblical history.

One reason Nebuchadnezzar may have exiled this large contingent to Babylon was to deprive Zedekiah of his best and brightest leaders and craftsmen, hoping to prevent further rebellions. But if that was the case, this strategy did not work. After eleven years of rule, Zedekiah rebelled, too. What happened next was the final fall of Jerusalem:

> In Zedekiah's ninth year as king, on the tenth day of the tenth month, King Nebuchadnezzar of Babylonia led his entire army to attack Jerusalem. . . . After a year and a half, all the food in Jerusalem was gone. Then on the ninth day of the fourth month, the Babylonia troops broke through the city wall. . . . [the commander of the Babylonian army] burned down the Lord's temple, the king's palace, and every important building in the city, as well as all houses. Then he ordered the Babylonia soldiers to break down the walls around Jerusalem. He led away as prisoners the people left in the city . . . Only some of the poorest people were left behind to work the vineyards and the fields. (2 Kings 25:1–12)

EXILE TO BABYLON

The Jewish people now found themselves in the demoralized position of walking some nine hundred miles to the very place that God had led their ancestor, Abraham—the founder of their nation—out of so many centuries before. Daniel was among them, separated from his parents, his homeland, and everything he had ever known. The people whom God had formed a special relationship and covenant with had been terribly disobedient, and their ungodly actions showed that they no longer acknowledged God as the source of all life, meaning, and success.

With all seemingly lost and facing seventy years of captivity in a foreign country, the people of Judah were now left with only their memories, which they turned into songs. One of their most famous songs, or Psalms, begins,

> By the rivers of Babylon,
> There we sat down, yea, we wept,
> When we remembered Zion.
> Upon the willow trees in the midst of that land
> We hanged up our harps.
>
> For there they that led us captive asked us to sing;
> And they that wanted us asked us to be glad, saying,
> 'Sing us one of the songs of Zion.'
> How shall we sing the Lord's song
> In a foreign land?

This 19th-century book illustration depicts the exiled Israelites weeping by the rivers of Babylon. "My mountain in the land and your wealth and all your treasures I will give away as plunder, together with your high places, because of sin throughout your country," God commands the prophet Jeremiah to tell the Israelites. "Through your own fault you will lose the inheritance I gave you. I will enslave you to your enemies in a land you do not know, for you have kindled my anger, and it will burn forever" (Jeremiah 17:3–4).

A WISE YOUNG MAN

Among the captured Israelites, however, was one right-eous young man. Though no more than about fourteen years old, Daniel was a standout, in the same way that his ancestor Abraham had been when he lived among the idol-worshipping Chaldeans of Mesopotamia. This Jewish youth of outstanding wisdom and piety would become a role model for his people, in how to do the will of God—come what may.

Though he didn't know it, Daniel was about to face a series of tests, including attempts to brainwash and indoc-trinate him into believing that the Babylonians' pagan ways were the right way to go.

Ultimately, Daniel will receive appointments to top-ranking positions among the Babylonians—he'll serve in the administration of three kings. He'll also prove that he is more than able to rise above his circumstances, and lead an uncompromising life, because of one simple truth: Daniel understands clearly that if he is to prosper in the world, he must learn to attribute his success to God—the giver of all knowledge, wisdom, reason, and intellect.

LIFE IN BABYLON

Babylon is the place where Daniel came as a teenager and would stay until he was past eighty. The Babylonians were a powerful, wealthy people, and their city was one of the most magnificent in the world. Located on a branch of the Euphrates River southwest of Baghdad in present-day Iraq, Babylon was the capital of Mesopotamia.

At the time, Babylon was not only the largest city in Mesopotamia but the largest metropolis in the world, measuring more than 340 square miles. The Greek philosopher Aristotle said it was as big as a nation, "for when Babylon was captured, it took many of its citizens three days to learn the news." No one knows for sure how many people lived there, but the historian Marc Van de Mieroop has written that "Mesopotamia was . . . the most densely urbanized region in the ancient world."

Babylon was laid out in the shape of a square, and a wall, measuring 60 miles in length (15 miles on each side) surrounded the city. In the walls were 250 guard towers and 100 solid brass gates that allowed entrance to and from the city. What's more, the walls were 300 feet high and 80 feet thick. The area inside the walls was about 200 square miles, which is nearly the size of New York City today.

A half-mile-long processional street led to the largest of eight gates, the Ishtar Gate; it was named for a Babylonian goddess symbolized by the lion. The glazed brick walls of the processional street were decorated with 120 lions and 575 dragons.

The Euphrates flowed from north to south through the middle of the city, with palm trees along the banks of the river. The streets of Babylon were paved with stone slabs, and fortifying the city was a defensive moat, both deep and wide, filled with water from the Euphrates. A draw-

Mesopotamia

Mesopotamia is a Greek name meaning "between the rivers," and refers to the land between the Tigris and Euphrates, roughly the northern and western borders of present-day Iraq. At different times in history it has been home to the civilizations and empires of Sumer, Babylonia, and Assyria. In the Old Testament of the Bible, Mesopotamia is known by several Hebrew names: Aram (Judges 3:8–11); Aram-Naharaim (Genesis 21:10; Deuteronomy 23:4; 1 Chronicles 19:6), and Padam-Aram. In Acts 2:9 and Acts 7:2 in the New Testament the word Mesopotamia is used. Mesopotamia was about the size of modern-day France.

bridge one-half mile in length and 30 feet wide was raised to close the city at night.

Homes in Babylon were made of bricks adorned with blue, yellow, or white tiles. When modern archaeologists later found these bricks, nearly all were inscribed with the words, "I am Nebuchadnezzar, King of Babylon." One inscription even recalled his boast in Daniel 4:30: "The fortifications of Esagila [Marduk's temple] and Babylon I strengthened and established the name of my reign forever."

In the center of the city stood a gleaming terraced tower in honor of the Babylonian god, Marduk. The Greek traveler and historian Herodotus described it:

> There was a tower of solid masonry, a little over 600 feet in length and width, upon which was raised a second tower, and on that third, and so on up to eight. The ascent to the top is outside, buy a path which winds round all the towers. When one is about half-way up, one finds a resting-place and seats, where persons are wont to sit some time on their way to the summit. On the topmost tower is a spacious temple, and inside the temple stands a couch of unusual size, richly adored with a golden table beside it.

The purpose of the ziggurat may have been for people to get closer to their gods—or for the gods to get closer to their people.

In all, there were 53 temples to various pagan gods in Babylon. The largest was dedicated to the god Bel; inside this temple, the golden idol of Bel and a golden table together weighed 25 tons. At the top of the Great Temple of Bel were golden images of Bel, Ishtar, two golden lions, a golden table 40 feet long and 15 feet wide, and another figure of solid gold 18 feet high.

View of the ornate Ishtar Gate of Babylon, decorated with lions, dragons, and other creatures.

The sun sets over the ruins of a Mesopotamian ziggurat. These enormous structures were constructed as temples to the gods worshipped in Babylon.

In fact, gold was everywhere in Babylon. When Herodotus visited the city a hundred or so years after Nebuchadnezzar's reign, he wrote that he had never imagined that so much gold existed.

"Mesopotamia is the birthplace of architecture," noted art historian Sigfried Giedion in his book *The Eternal Present*. "The age-old yearning to establish contact with invisible forces was, for the first time, given an architectural form.

Nebuchadnezzar himself delighted in the architecture of Babylon, describing it as "the marvel of mankind, the center of the land, shining residence, the dwelling of majesty."

NEBUCHADNEZZAR

For much of the first three decades of his reign, Nebuchadnezzar was preoccupied with warfare. He led his armies to defeat many cities including Tyre, and desolated Moab, Ammon, Edom, and Lebanon, in addition to Jerusalem. People thought of him as the mightiest warrior of his day, and the most distinguished ruler of the Neo-Babylonian (Chaldean) dynasty.

He was married to a Median princess named Amyhia, and built for her the famous Hanging Gardens of Babylon, considered by the Greeks as one of the seven wonders of the ancient world. Amyhia was homesick for the green mountains of her homeland. So Nebuchadnezzar had an artificial mountain made with tiers where trees (oak, pine, willow, ash, orange, pomegranate, and palm) and other green plants grew. As the plants became large, they grew over the edge of the tiers, so that they seemed to "hang"

Modern digital illustration of the famed Hanging Gardens of Babylon, based on ancient accounts. The Hanging Gardens were considered one of the seven wonders of the ancient world.

Detail of a dragon from the Ishtar Gate. The dragon was a representation of Marduk, the patron deity of Babylon. His main sanctuary, the Esagila, was located in Babylon. In Babylonian mythology, Marduk was a champion of good over evil. The Akkadian word Bel, meaning "lord" or "master," was often applied to Marduk in ancient times.

there. The plants were watered by a system of chains and buckets that lifted water to the top of each tier. Nebuchadnezzar's palace covered seven acres and had five courtyards, and a throne room measuring about 50 feet by 150 feet—one quarter the size of a football field. One wall of the throne room had a design of blue enameled bricks, but the other three were covered in white alabaster.

DANIEL AND HIS THREE FRIENDS

When the Hebrew captives were brought to the land of Chaldea, or Babylon, King Nebuchadnezzar instructed the highest-ranking official in his palace, Ashpenaz, to find the best and brightest young men among them. Specifically, the king ordered Ashpenaz, the master of his eunuchs, to bring in "children in whom was no blemish, but well favored, and skillful in all wisdom, and cunning in knowledge, and understanding science, and such as had ability in them to stand in the king's palace, and whom they might teach the learning and the tongue of the Chaldeans" (Daniel 1:3–4).

He further instructed Ashpenaz, "to teach them how to speak and write our language and give them the same food and wine that I am served. Train them for three years, and then they can become court officials" (Daniel 1:4, 5).

The chosen four were Daniel and his friends. Once selected, the king's chief official gave them Babylonian names: Daniel became Belteshazzar, which means "Bel's prince," Hananiah became Shadrach, which may be a corruption of the god-name "Marduk," Mishael became

An example of Akkadian cuneiform writing can be seen on this clay tablet found in Mesopotamia. To learn how to read and write Akkadian, the language used in the court of ancient Babylon, a student had to memorize hundreds of wedge-shaped characters.

Meshach, a name for which there is no clear scholarly explanation, and Azariah became Abednego, which is most likely a corruption of "Abed-Nego" (servant of Nego or Nebo; among the Chaldeans Nebo was the terms used for the planet Mercury, which they worshipped).

The changing of the youths' names marked the beginning of a sustained effort by Nebuchadnezzar to brainwash Daniel and his friends. Perhaps the thinking behind the king's decision was this: if the youths could forget their country and religion, maybe they would instead pledge their loyalty to him. And if this happened, perhaps it would encourage all Jewish people to adopt Babylonian customs and ways. This form of mind control is a practice that was not uncommon in that era and neither is it today. It remains a feature of war, as many prisoners of war have attested.

But there may have been another reason, besides indoctrination, why Nebuchadnezzar wanted the best minds among the Jews.

The Babylonians studied astronomy and even had stargazers who watched the skies throughout the night. Archaeologists have discovered the records of these stargazers and how they recorded the movements of the heavenly bodies. They were especially interested in astrology, magic, soothsaying, and divination—sciences that helped them predict future events, interpret dreams, or help them to figure out the secrets of the invisible world. Some Bible commentators have speculated that Nebuchadnezzar may have sought out the wisest Israelite youths, because he wanted to know what the Hebrews knew in regards to science.

On the surface, the Babylonian lifestyle may have seemed enticing to some of the Hebrew captives. After all, it was a society of luxury and grandeur. However, Daniel

In ancient Babylon, science embraced everything from music and moral theology to astronomy, astrology, and sorcery.

was resolute in his Jewish faith. While he couldn't refuse the name change, Daniel made up his mind to eat and drink only what God had approved for his people to eat. And there were many restrictions on the Jewish diet. Pork and certain kinds of fish were forbidden, for example. Wine was not forbidden by Jewish law; and, it can be assumed that Nebuchadnezzar had the best selections of wine, since he was the world's most powerful man. However, excessive drinking can lead to drunkenness, and irrational thoughts and behavior, and Daniel simply decided to exercise restraint.

When the time came for Daniel to eat the food and drink the wine from the king's table, he asked Ashpenaz for an alternative menu. But Ashpenaz was afraid: "The king has decided what you must eat and drink. And I am afraid he will kill me, if you eat something else and end up looking worse than the other young men." (Daniel 1:10).

This time Daniel went to the guard whom the chief official had appointed to oversee the captives. He asked the guard to let him and his friends eat a vegetarian diet for ten days. They would eat vegetables, fruits, grains, and seeds—anything grown in the soil. Then Daniel and his friends told the guard, "'compare our appearance with that of the young men who eat the royal food, and treat your servants in accordance with what you see'" (Daniel 1:13).

After ten days, the four Jewish youths looked far better in appearance than their non-Jewish companions, so the guard made this a permanent diet for Daniel, Meshach, Shadrach, and Abednego.

In a distant land, far from his parents, and his temple, and in the midst of temptations, Daniel had shown moral bravery and courage, by refusing to eat the king's food and to drink his wine.

He had also impressed the king, but more importantly, he had found favor with God for staying true to the dietary laws of the Jewish people. The Jewish diet was part and parcel of a lifestyle that God expected His people to follow.

For his show of faith, integrity, and loyalty, God blessed Daniel and his friends. He gave them knowledge and understanding of all kinds of literature and learning, and to Daniel he gave one extra special gift: the ability to understand visions and dreams.

At the end of the three years of training, all the Israelite captives were brought before King Nebuchadnezzar, who found Daniel and his friends to be the most impressive. "[He] found none like Daniel, Hananiah, Mishael, and Azariah; therefore stood they before the king. And in all matters of wisdom and understanding, that the king enquired of them, he found them ten times better than all the magicians and astrologers that were in all his realm" (Daniel 1:19, 20).

NIGHT TERRORS SHAKE THE KING

One of Daniel's first challenges in dream interpretation came when King Nebuchadnezzar began having nightmares. No matter how hard the king tried to sleep, he awakened in a cold sweat, with heart-pounding fear. As time passed, the king became more and more troubled. Sleep deprivation caused him to become paranoid, and quick to anger.

The Babylonians believed that their gods sent visions or messages through dreams, and Nebuchadnezzar believed that his dreams had special meaning. He assembled all the wisest people in Babylon—his magicians, psychics, interpreters, and astrologers. He asked them to tell him not only the meaning of the dream, but the dream itself. Bible commentators have speculated that perhaps Nebuchadnezzar could not remember what the dream was about when awake. Alternatively, maybe he remembered the dream but wanted to test

41

his counselors and soothsayers to be certain of the accuracy of their explanations. Either way, it was of great importance to the king to find out the meaning of his dreams, so much so that he threatened those assembled with dire punishments: he would take their lives and destroy their homes, if they were wrong, or give them gifts and rewards, if correct in their interpretations.

But the sages were not up to the task. They explained to the king that it would be impossible for any man to do what he had asked of them. They admitted that it was above their ability saying, "There is not a man on earth who can do what the king asks! No king, however great and mighty, has ever asked such a thing of any magician or enchanter or astrologer. What the king asks is too difficult. No one can reveal it to the King except the gods, and they do not live among men.'" (Daniel 2:10–11)

Enraged, Nebuchadnezzar ordered the slaughter of all his wise men; the order put Daniel and his friends in harm's way, too, because the king had examined the young men to see if they were fit for service, and found them ten times wiser than all the rest in his court. So when the decree went out from King Nebuchadnezzar to kill all the wise men, it included Daniel, Hananiah, Mishael, and Azariah.

DANIEL AND ARIOCH

Arioch was the captain of the royal guard. Daniel went to him to discover the details of the king's rash and cruel decision to carry out a mass execution. Daniel used carefully measured words and spoke tactfully with Arioch, who explained the situation.

Daniel then met with his faithful friends. He explained to them the need to pray that God would reveal the mystery of the King's dream. The four friends prayed and then retired to their beds. That night God revealed to Daniel the mystery and meaning of Nebuchadnezzar's dream, and Daniel thanked God in a prayer:

> Praise be to the name of God for ever and ever;
>   wisdom and power are his.
> He changes times and seasons;
> He sets up kings and deposes them.
> He gives wisdom to the wise and knowledge
>   to the discerning.
> He reveals deep and hidden things;
> He knows what lies in darkness, and light dwells
>   with him.
> I thank and praise you,
> O God of my fathers:
> You have given me wisdom and power,
> you have made known to me what we asked
>   of you,
> you have made known to us the dream of the
>   king (Daniel 2:20–23).

David returned to Arioch, with the news that he would be able to interpret the mystery of the king's dream. Arioch brought David to the king immediately and said, "'I have found a man among the exiles from Judah who can tell the king what his dream means" (Daniel 2:25).

DANIEL EXPLAINS THE KING'S DREAM

When Daniel was presented to King Nebuchadnezzar, Daniel said, "No wise man, enchanter, magician or diviner can explain to the king the mystery he has asked about, but there is a God in heaven who reveals mysteries" (Daniel 2:27–28). He further explained that the dream was not an ordinary one. It was a vision of things to come.

Daniel told the king that he had dreamt of a giant-sized statue of a man. It glimmered brightly in the sun and was remarkable in its appearance. Designed to look like a person, each part of the body was made from a different material. The head of the statue was pure gold. The chest and the arms were silver. The abdomen and the thighs were bronze. Finally, at the bottom of the statue were legs of iron. The feet and toes were of iron and baked clay. In the dream, while the king stared at the statue, an unusual rock, one that human hands could not have cut, struck the statue at the feet and destroyed it. "This was the dream, and now we will interpret it to the king" (Daniel 2:36).

THE DREAM'S MEANING

The meaning Daniel was about to reveal would not hold good news for the king. He began by acknowledging that King Nebuchadnezzar was a powerful ruler: "You, O king, are the king of kings. The God of heaven has given you dominion and power and might and glory; in your hands, he has placed mankind and the beasts of the field and the birds of the air. Wherever they live, he has made you ruler over them all" (Daniel 2:37–38).

Then he proceeded to tell him that it was not the pagan gods that allowed him to rule, but the God of Israel. Daniel explained that the gold head of the statue symbolized King Nebuchadnezzar's kingdom. The other parts of the statue symbolized future kingdoms that would defeat him.

The silver, which made up the chest and arms, symbolized a second kingdom that would be established by a weaker government. This kingdom would come and defeat Babylon. The next part of the body, the bronze belly and thighs, symbolized a third empire. It would be a government that would be inferior to the silver. The fourth kingdom, symbolized by the legs of iron and feet of iron and clay, would be a seemingly powerful government. But it,

An interpretation of Nebuchadnezzar's dream of the giant statue at Gilgal Sculpture Garden, Utah. Historically, Bible scholars have identified the golden head with the Babylonian Empire, the silver arms and chest with the Persian Empire, which conquered Babylon in 539 B.C.E., the copper belly and thighs with the Greeks, who conquered Persia in 330 B.C.E., and the iron legs with the Roman Empire, which had gained control over most of the Greek states by the first century B.C.E.

too, would be someday defeated. The fifth kingdom, or the last part of the statue, was the feet and toes that were made of iron and clay. They symbolized a kingdom that was half strong and half brittle. It would be a strong government, but it would have weaknesses and be easily broken.

In the last part of the dream, there was a rock. It had a special quality and had not been cut by a human. This rock obliterated the statue. It turned the statue into chaff, like that found on the floor of a threshing room. This was a picture the king could understand and would have seen.

Threshing was a process used to separate the good grain from the uneatable chaff. Wheat stalks were threshed by having oxen walk over them or drag a heavy stone over them. The grain was then thrown into the air. A papery husk called chaff would then blow away in the wind. Chaff was considered worthless. It was like dust. Thus, the king's dream ended with the impressive statue being blown away like dust.

Daniel explained that the rock that crushed the statue and grew to fill the whole earth symbolized one final kingdom that God would establish. The ruler would not be earthly people but God himself. This final kingdom would last forever.

KING NEBUCHADNEZZAR'S REACTION

Daniel made it very clear to King Nebuchadnezzar that God had shown him what was to take place in the future. He explained that God, who had sent the dream, was reliable and King Nebuchadnezzar had no reason to doubt the meaning.

Overwhelmed with emotion, King Nebuchadnezzar fell to his knees and bowed in front of Daniel. Kings did not bow down to others, especially not to a captive servant. Kings usually have people bow before them. But this was more than bowing to a captive slave; this was the king recognizing and declaring God's power. "Surely your God is the God of gods and the Lord of kings and a revealer of mysteries, for you were able to reveal this mystery" (Daniel 2:47).

So grateful was King Nebuchadnezzar that he lavished gifts upon Daniel as a reward, and he made him chief of all the advisors whose lives he had saved. Daniel's friends, Hananiah, Mishael, and Azariah, also were appointed to high positions in the Babylonian administration.

FACING THE FIERY FURNACE

Outside the city of Babylon, on the plain of Dura, Nebuchadnezzar had a colossal gold statue erected. What year this happened is a matter of speculation; and the Bible does not state in whose honor the image was made. In some Greek and Arabic translations of the Book of Daniel, the year is said to have been in the eighteenth year of Nebuchadnezzar's reign, but this is not universally accepted among Biblical scholars.

One of the most remarkable features of this structure was its unusual proportions. It was ninety feet high, or about nine stories tall, and nine feet wide. Monuments made with this type of architectural design are called obelisks. They are tall and slender with four sides that become narrower at the top. Many times they are made of a single block of stone. King Nebuchadnezzar covered his obelisk with gold, and it was meant to be an object of worship.

THE KING'S DECREE

When completed, the king called together every important person in Babylon to dedicate the statue. His guest list included eight types of officials—satraps, special governors who ruled over a distinct region; prefects, high-ranking administrative officials who worked under the satraps; governors, who ruled smaller regions; advisors, the men who counseled the king on various matters, including the military; treasurers, who were the overseers of the king's finances; judges, who settled disputes among the inhabitants of Babylon; magistrates, who were Babylon's police force or sheriffs, and finally, provincial officials, who were

The seal of Nebuchadnezzar, shown here, would have been included on any royal communication or decree. The Biblical name Nebuchadnezzar represents the Jewish form of the Babylonian name Nebuchadrezzar. His name is also spelled Nabu-kudurri-usur, which translated means "the (god) Nabu has protected my succession (or boundary)."

similar to mayors. All were summoned to assemble at the statue for the dedication.

In those days, Babylonians sent messages using a herald. A herald was a person whose duty it was to shout a message or news from the king. When the king made a new decree or law, a herald would go throughout the country and shout out what the new law was. A herald could usually speak two or more languages so that everyone who heard the message could understand it in their own language. On the day of the dedication of the statue, a herald proclaimed, "This is what you are commanded to do, O peoples, nations and men of every language: As soon as you hear the sound of the horn, flute, zither, lyre, harp, pipes and all kinds of music, you must fall down and worship the image of gold that King Nebuchadnezzar has set up. Whoever does not fall down and worship will immediately be thrown into a blazing furnace" (Daniel 3:4–6).

Everyone present bowed, as the herald had instructed, except for Daniel's friends, who remained standing. Daniel was not present for the dedication, and the Bible does not provide an explanation for where he may have been. But this act of defiance by Daniel's friends, as it must have been perceived, did not go unnoticed by some Babylonians. "There are some Jews whom you have set over the affairs of the province of Babylon—Shadrach, Meshach and Abednego—who pay no attention to you, O king. They neither serve your gods nor worship the image of gold you have set up'" (Daniel 3:12).

Not surprisingly, there were many who resented the elevated status of the Hebrew captives and wanted the king to punish them. Specifically, they wanted the Israelites thrown into a furnace.

Nebuchadnezzar called the three men to come before him. "Is it true, Shadrach, Meshach and Abednego, that you do not serve my gods or worship the image of gold I have set up?" (Daniel 3:14) The king offered the men a way out of their punishment. He asked if they would be willing to bow down when they heard the music play from this time on. But, if they still would not bow down, then they would have to face the fiery furnace immediately. Respectfully, the three refused; even if they were frightened, they had made a firm decision to live by the laws of God.

These Hebrew friends had firmly resolved years earlier to put God first; they demonstrated this loyalty when they refused to eat from the king's table. Now, again, they firmly resolved to be loyal to their God and not worship the graven image. They didn't care what happened to them next—wealth or poverty, life or death, honor or dishonor, high position or no position. Their minds were firmly fixed on doing what they believed was morally right, in the eyes of God. After all, idolatry is one of the sins that had led to the Israelites exile in Babylon.

Shadrach, Meshach, and Abednego also believed that God would deliver them. "O Nebuchadnezzar," they said, "we do not need to defend ourselves before you in this matter. If we are thrown into the blazing furnace, the God we serve is able to save us from it, and he will rescue us from your hand, O king. But even if he does not, we want you to know, O king, that we will not serve your gods or worship the image of gold you have set up" (Daniel 3:16–18).

Nebuchadnezzar became enraged, and ordered that the furnace be made seven times hotter than usual. The furnace in question may have been one used to bake bricks or melt gold. A series of bellows controlled the heat. Bellows are mechanisms used to force air into the furnace, increasing the flames and the heat inside the furnace.

sye werden im nit anhangen als das eysen nit
mag werden vermischet mit dē scherben. Aber
in den tagen diser reich got des hymels wirt er
fücken ein reich. Es da nit wirt verwüstet ewigk

das volck Sy anbetten solt. Da aber sydrack mit
sac vnd abdenago. Die nit anbetten wolte, So
wurden sy in einen glüenden ofen gesetzet.

This woodcut from an illustrated Bible of the 15th century shows Shadrach, Meshach, and Abednego in the fiery furnace. The flames are so hot that they are consuming the men who threw the Hebrews into the fire.

The king ordered the strongest men of his army to tie up Shadrach, Meshach, and Abednego to remind them that they were helpless to save themselves. The fire was so hot that it killed the men, as they cast Shadrach, Meshach, and Abednego into the fire.

MIRACLE IN THE FIERY FURNACE

Many people had come to watch what would happen to Shadrach, Meshach, and Abednego. The audience included the king, satraps, prefects, governors, and royal advisors. But they did not see what they expected. Inside the flaming furnace, Shadrach, Meshach, and Abednego were walking around unharmed with a fourth person. The shocked king leapt up from his seat to exclaim, "Weren't there three men that we tied up and threw into the fire? . . . Look! I see four men walking around in the fire, unbound and unharmed, and the fourth looks like a son of the gods" (Daniel 3:24–25).

The king could not believe his eyes. He walked near the opening of the furnace and called out, "'Shadrach, Meshach and Abednego, servants of the Most High God, come out! Come here!'" (Daniel 3:26). When the three walked out of the furnace, they were not harmed in any way. Their hair was not singed from the flames. They did not even smell of smoke.

Through the Flames

Who was the mysterious fourth man who walked through the flames with Shadrach, Meshach, and Abednego? This is a question that Biblical scholars have debated for centuries. Some Christians believe that the fourth person was the preincarnate Christ, not an angel. Jesus Christ is the central figure in the New Testament, and Christians believe that He is both God incarnate and a human being. According to the scriptures, in times of tribulation God's own are assured of His presence and deliverance.

After this incident, Nebuchadnezzar confessed his faith in the Hebrew God—this marked the second time—and he issued a new decree. The new decree declared that no one would be allowed to speak against the God of Shadrach, Meshach, and Abednego. The Hebrew men would now be free to worship their God without fear of punishment. Furthermore, the king was so amazed at the men's faithfulness to their God, he promoted them to higher positions in Babylon. Shadrach, Meshach, and Abednego, saved by God from the fire, once again prospered in the land of Babylon.

FAITH BY FIRE

For readers today, the story of these three friends is almost too hard to believe. After all, who can survive such a fire? And what exactly is the point of the story? Many rabbis and ministers of the gospel would say that this particular narrative is about the power of faith. Shadrach, Meshach, and Abednego are so strong in their faith in God and what He can and will do for them that they are without fear.

Imagine having that fearless attitude in all situations—moving to a new town, making new friends, starting a new job, dealing with difficult people, saying no to vices that could harm you, even though everyone around you may say that doing these things is okay. Thankfully, we do not live in an age where people are thrown into fiery furnaces as punishment. Nevertheless, people do face "fires" in their lives—fires in the sense that one's convictions, integrity, ethics, morals, and faith are tested. The question is, will we pass the test?

In his book, *Luck, A Secular Faith*, Wayne Edward Oates writes that faith has taken a back seat to luck in contemporary life. "Many people worship luck, fate, fortune, chance, or the odds. This blind allegiance to faith probably has ancient origins."

Oates adds that "the opposite of this belief is luck, odds, and chances is faith like that affirmed by Shadrach, Meshach, and Abednego in their response to Nebuchadnezzar's threat to put them in the fiery furnace if they did not bow down and worship his pagan god."

STRANGE DREAMS
AND WRITINGS

I t is now a time of peace and prosperity in Babylon. The
Babylonians are focused on their art, culture, and com-
pleting building projects, and the king is without
worry. He is living a grand life of luxury; that is, until he
begins, once again, to have horrifying dreams and visions.

About thirty years had passed since he had been
plagued by those other night terrors. He first called
together his wise men—the court magicians, enchanters,
astrologers, and soothsayers. But they could not interpret
his dream. Then he called Daniel.

"I know that the spirit of the holy gods is in
you, and no mystery is too difficult for you,"
the king told Daniel (Daniel 4:9). Then he
explained the dream. He told Daniel that
he saw an enormous oak tree. It grew in
the middle of the earth. The tree grew so
large that it could be seen by everyone in
the whole world. The tree flourished and
had beautiful leaves. Lots of delicious fruit

grew from its branches and fed all the people. Wild animals enjoyed living in its shade, and birds made nests in its branches.

Suddenly, the dream changed. A messenger from heaven appeared in the vision. This holy being called in a loud voice, "Cut down the tree and trim off its branches; strip off its leaves and scatter its fruit. Let the animals flee from under it and the birds from its branches" (Daniel 4:14). Then the messenger said to leave the roots and the stump of the tree wrapped in iron and bronze. Next the messenger said something that was difficult to understand. He said to let the heart of the man become like the heart of a beast for seven years.

The messenger proclaimed that this should happen so that all of the world would know that God Almighty has power over every living creature. The world would know that God's rule is sovereign even over the most powerful and mighty rulers of the earth.

DANIEL EXPLAINS THE DREAM
OF THE OAK TREE

When King Nebuchadnezzar finished telling Daniel the dream, he asked for an interpretation. At first the dream stunned Daniel. He realized why the dream would be disturbing to the King Nebuchadnezzar. The king coaxed Daniel, "do not let the dream or its meaning alarm you" (Daniel 4:19). Daniel told the king that the dream's meaning was so terrible, that he wished the events prophesied by the dream would happen to the king's enemies and not to the king himself. Nevertheless, he revealed its meaning.

"The tree you saw, which grew large and strong, with its top touching the sky, visible to the whole earth, with beautiful leaves and abundant fruit, providing food for all, giving shelter to the beasts of the field, and having nesting

Nebuchadnezzar's dream of the tree foretold the king's impending fall from power.

places in its branches for the birds of the air—you, O king, are that tree! You have become great and strong; your greatness has grown until it reaches the sky, and your dominion extends to distant parts of the earth" (Daniel 4:20–22).

Nebuchadnezzar would have been pleased to hear the first part of the dream's interpretation. However, the next part would have surely been disturbing to him.

King Nebuchadnezzar had seen a messenger, an angel from heaven come down to earth. The messenger from God said, "Cut down the tree and destroy it" (Daniel 4:23). Only a stump of the tree will be left, but the stump will be bound. Then in Chapter 4, verse 15, the stump suddenly becomes a person. This person will live in the fields where dew will gather on him, and his mind is to be changed from that of a man to a beast for seven years.

Daniel explained that the dream meant that King Nebuchadnezzar would be removed from the palace. He would live in the fields like an animal. For food, he would eat grass. The king would live like this for seven years, until Nebuchadnezzar recognized that it was God who made him great and not King Nebuchadnezzar himself. Daniel added that the king would not die, but that he would return to his throne to reign again. This time King Nebuchadnezzar would honor God as Supreme Ruler over all creation.

DANIEL COUNSELS THE KING

Daniel counseled the king that it was not too late to change his ways and avoid the dream's prediction. All these things would happen because the king was prideful; he thought he was greater than God. Daniel advised the king to repent from his self-indulgent and selfish practices.

King Nebuchadnezzar refused to listen to Daniel's advice, and for the next year, he lived in the palace doing as he pleased. Then one day Nebuchadnezzar was strolling on the roof of the palace when he boasted, saying aloud, "Is not this the great Babylon I have built as the royal residence, by my mighty power and for the glory of my majesty?" (Daniel 4:30)

The king had barely finished speaking when he heard the voice of God, "This is what is decreed for you, King Nebuchadnezzar: your royal authority has been taken from you. You will be driven away from people and will live with the wild animals; you will eat grass like cattle. Seven times will pass by for you until you acknowledge that the Most High is sovereign over the kingdoms of men and gives them to anyone he wishes" (Daniel 4:31–32). From that point on, Nebuchadnezzar suffered with temporary mental derangement (lycanthropy), a condition in which the victim imagines himself to be a wild beast.

The king's associates banished him from the palace because his thinking had become jumbled. For the next seven years Nebuchadnezzar, who had experienced the best of everything, lived with the wild animals, ate grass to survive, and slept on the ground.

SANITY RETURNS

God did not allow the king to die, though. Instead, King Nebuchadnezzar changed. After seven years, he accepted God as sovereign. The king looked up to heaven and

This watercolor painting (circa 1795) by the English poet, illustrator, and publisher William Blake depicts Nebuchadnezzar in his madness. Nebuchadnezzar's madness is one of the stories in the Book of Daniel that has long troubled Christian and Jewish scholars. Some contend that it was actually Nabonidus, who ruled after Nebuchadnezzar, who spent time in the desert. In fact, a Dead Sea Scroll text identifies Nabonidus as the king with a mental malady. Other scholars, meanwhile, maintain that this particular story is simply fictitious.

praised the Most High God, thanking Him for all his possessions and power.

After Nebuchadnezzar's sanity had returned, and he had confessed his faith, God restored him to the throne, and his kingdom was even greater than before. God blessed Nebuchadnezzar with more wealth and power. "Now I, Nebuchadnezzar praise and exalt and glorify the King of heaven, because everything he does is right and all his ways are just. And those who walk in pride he is able to humble" (Daniel 4:37).

Nebuchadnezzar lived his last days in sincere and honest worship of the God of Israel. But after his death came a new king, who did not honor God. Once again, Daniel found himself in a dangerous situation.

The Story of Susanna

In Roman Catholic editions of the Bible the story of Susanna appears as Chapter 13. The narrative is about a beautiful woman named Susanna, who is the wife of a wealthy and respected Jew named Joakim. She walks daily in the garden, and two Jewish elders begin to burn with lust for her. They devise a plan to get her alone, and then threaten her when she refuses to have sex with them.

But Susanna cries out for help. The elders accuse her of adultery, and she is forced to stand trial. Her penalty, if found guilty, is death. But Daniel intervenes, and he rebukes the Israelites for condemning Susanna without sufficient evidence. During cross-examination in court, Daniel succeeds in exposing the two elders for telling lies. Susanna is found innocent, and thereafter, Daniel's reputation as a hero and wise man grew among the Hebrew people.

Some Biblical scholars believe that this story has no basis in fact. Instead, they see it has an example of the kind of Jewish literature that made Daniel a hero. It illustrates the high regard people had for Daniel.

THE LAST BANQUET OF BABYLON

Nebuchadnezzar ruled to 562 B.C.E. His only son Amel-Marduk (also called Evil-Merodach) succeeded him and reigned for two years. During his short reign, he released King Jehoiachin and treated him as a royal foreign guest.

Amel-Marduk was murdered by his brother-in-law Nergal-Sharezer, and Nergal-Sharezer was succeeded by his young son Labashi-Marduk in 556 B.C.E. The boy was murdered shortly after his ascension by Nabonidus. Nabonidus married one of Nebuchadnezzar's daughters, and they had a son named Belshazzar.

Nabonidus, for reasons unknown, chose not to make Babylon his capital. Instead, he resided in Tema of Arabia. He appointed his son Belshazzar to become co-regent with him of Babylon.

Chapter 5 of the Book of Daniel begins with King Belshazzar, who is hosting a great banquet for a thousand of his nobles. But this is a particularly inappropriate time to be celebrating because the armies of Persia and Mede were trying to invade Babylon. Months earlier the Persians and the Medes had captured Belshazzar's father, Nabonidus.

Meanwhile, Daniel has been in Babylon for some seventy years, which means he was about eighty-four years old. Though well known and respected by past Babylonia kings for giving sound advice, Belshazzar did not seek his counsel.

Indeed, Belshazzar was not concerned about his father's capture, he was not concerned about the enemy attacking, nor was he concerned about duties of kingship. He was only concerned about having a great feast.

While Belshazzar was enjoying his celebration, he ordered some servants to bring in the gold and silver goblets that Nebuchadnezzar had taken from Solomon's Temple in Jerusalem at the time he deported the Hebrew captives. Nebuchadnezzar had stored the goblets in the temple of the Babylonian gods, and they had stayed there until the day of Belshazzar's banquet.

The gold and silver goblets had an important meaning for the Hebrew people. The ancestors of the Hebrews had consecrated or blessed these utensils for their use only in the temple. Consecration separated ordinary and common items, such as the goblets, and signified that they were now items devoted exclusively for use in the worship of God.

The servants obeyed, and Belshazzar and his wives and concubines drank from the goblets. They used the full goblets to praise the pagan gods of Babylon.

"Suddenly," according to the scriptures, "the fingers of a human hand appeared and wrote on the plaster of the wall, near the lamp stand in the royal palace. The king watched the hand as it wrote. His face turned pale and he

The Dutch master Rembrandt painted this scene of Belshazzar's feast. Archaeologists have found evidence that King Belshazzar was a real person. Henry H. Halley writes, "In 1853 an inscription was found on the cornerstone of a temple built by Nabonidas . . . which read: 'May I, Nabonidas, king of Babylon, not sin against thee. And may reverence for thee dwell in the heart of Belshazzar, my firstborn, favorite son.'"

was so frightened that his knees knocked together and his legs gave way" (Daniel 5:5, 6).

It was a common practice in antiquity for kings to write messages on the palace walls. They used it as a place to exalt themselves. They listed their victories, their titles, and their famous deeds. It was a way for them to pay tribute to themselves. But this message did not glorify the king; this message on the wall was unique.

The horrified king called for his advisors, enchanters, astrologers, and diviners. "Whoever reads this writing and tells me what it means will be clothed in purple and have a gold chain placed around his neck and he will be made the third highest ruler in the kingdom" (Daniel 5:7).

He offered rewards of the finest purple clothing, a gold necklace, and a high-ranking position. Specifically, he offered the empire's third highest-ranking position. The only people above that rank would have been King Belshazzar himself and his father, King Nabonidus.

But the wisest men of Babylon couldn't explain the words written by the mysterious hand. This made the king more terrified. His face became paler. All the nobles and advisors were frightened and confused at this strange message.

THE QUEEN REMEMBERS DANIEL

The queen heard the loud voices coming from the banquet hall. It was not King Belshazzar's wife because he had been feasting with his wives. This queen may have been the wife of his father, King Nabonidus, or perhaps his mother, Nitocris; then again, it may have been the aged widow of Nebuchadnezzar. In any event, the queen was a woman of prestige and was brave enough to enter the banquet hall without an invitation from the king.

When she arrived, she began to instruct him in what he needed to do. "Don't be alarmed! Don't look so pale!" she said. "There is a man in your kingdom who has the spirit

In Daniel's day, only the very rich wore the color purple. Purple dye was made from a species of shellfish in the Mediterranean Sea, and from the shells of sea snails. Needless to say, it took thousands of shells to make a small amount of purple dye. So only kings and other royalty, or the rich and influential, could afford to wear clothing this color.

of the holy gods in him" (Daniel 5:10). She explained to Belshazzar that Daniel had been appointed chief of the advisors by Nebuchadnezzar because of his vast wisdom. The queen continued, "This man Daniel, whom the king called Belteshazzar, was found to have a keen mind and knowledge and understanding, and also the ability to interpret dreams, explain riddles and solve difficult problems. Call for Daniel and he will tell you what the writing means" (Daniel 5:12). So Daniel was summoned to appear before the king.

The king explained to Daniel his problem: "The wise men and enchanters were brought before me to read this writing and tell me what it means, but they could not explain it. Now I have heard that you are able to give interpretations and to solve difficult problems" (Daniel 5:15–16). Then the king promised Daniel the gifts he had promised the other wise men—the purple clothing, a gold chain for his neck, and to be made the third-highest ruler in the kingdom—if he could read and interpret the secret message written on the wall of the banquet hall.

DANIEL AGREES TO HELP BELSHAZZAR

Daniel politely refused the gifts, "You may keep your gifts for yourself and give your rewards to someone else. Nevertheless, I will read the writing for the king and tell him what it means" (Daniel 5:17).

He then accused Belshazzar of not learning from the past. He reminded him of Nebuchadnezzar's pride and conceit, and the consequences of his arrogance.

> You had the goblets from his temple brought to you, and you and your nobles, your wives and your concubines drank wine from them. You praised the gods of silver and gold, of bronze, iron, wood and stone, which cannot see or hear or understand. But

Daniel interprets the mysterious message for King Belshazzar.

you did not honor the God who holds in his hand your life and all your ways. Therefore he sent the hand that wrote the inscription (Daniel 2:23–24).

THE MYSTERIOUS MESSAGE INTERPRETED

The inscription on the wall read: *Mene, Mene, Tekel, Parsin*. The words were written in Aramaic, the native tongue of the Babylonians. The king's advisors would have been able to read the words, but they could not understand the words' mysterious meaning. The wall that usually held flattery and praises for the king now told of his destruction. Daniel, with his God-given ability to interpret, explained the secret message.

The word *Mene* means "numbered." It meant that God had numbered the days of the Babylonian Empire because the king had no regard for God; God had numbered Belshazzar's days as ruler. God had determined that not only was this an end to King Belshazzar's days as ruler but also King Belshazzar's life. "Since they show no regard for the works of the Lord and what his hands have done, he will tear them down and never build them up again" (Psalms 28:5).

The word *Tekel* means "weighed." Weight is a measurement used to decide or judge the value of something. God had weighed or judged Belshazzar and found him to be worthless. King Belshazzar's downfall was a direct result of his failure to measure up to God's standards. The word *Parsin* means "divided." The last word of the inscription foretold the division of the Babylonian Kingdom.

THE END OF THE BABYLONIAN EMPIRE

On the night of King Belshazzar's elaborate feast, the powerful Persian army attacked Babylon. Babylon had strong defenses—its walls and moat fortified the city against invasion. But the invaders diverted the Euphrates River, which ran through the center of the city, into an alternate channel. The army, commanded by Cyrus the Great and guided by two Babylonian deserters, marched into the city through the dry riverbed and attacked. King Belshazzar was executed on that very night. Cyrus and the Persian army gained the victory over the Babylonians without a battle.

Babylon, the land that had been ruled by great kings and the city that the whole world praised, had been captured. The Babylonian Empire, symbolized in Nebuchadnezzar's dream as the head of gold, existed no more.

Babylon Lost and Found

There were two Babylonian Empires that existed in the ancient Near East. The first was the Old Babylonian Empire, a dominant world power from around 2000 to 1600 B.C.E. The kingdom in which Daniel lived was called the Neo-Babylonian (or Chaldean) Empire. This Babylonian empire, which included the city of Babylon, lasted from 625 to 539 B.C.E. The empire ceased to exist after it was conquered by the Persians and Medes. However, the city of Babylon remained an important center of trade and social activity until around 650 C.E.

During the late 19th and early 20th centuries, archaeologists began to excavate the ruins of Babylon.

Many have looked for clues or artifacts that would prove that events mentioned in the Bible really did occur and that people such as Daniel, Nebuchadnezzar, and Belshazzar truly did exist.

In her book *Daniel: Lives of Integrity, Words of Prophecy*, Beth Moore writes, "Archaeologists have excavated a large hall in Babylon 55 feet wide and 165 feet long that had plastered walls. . . . these archaeologists very likely excavated the same plaster walls that God once used for a chalkboard." A hall of this size would certainly have been large enough to hold a banquet feast the size of King Belshazzar's elaborate celebration.

IN THE
LIONS' LAIR

Daniel was an elderly man of about eighty-five years old when the Persians and Medes took control of Babylon. He had prospered and outlived several kings.

A 62-year-old Mede named Darius was now at the helm in Babylon. His duties were more of an administrator, but he had all the responsibilities and privileges of a king, so he was referred to as a king. Darius ruled under the authority of Cyrus the Great of Persia, who lived from 600 to 529 B.C.E.

The Persian Empire was vast; it had been growing in power and strength. First it conquered the country of Media in 553 B.C.E. Media was located about 400 miles north of the Persian Gulf. Then Persia and Media joined forces and conquered Babylon.

Darius began his reign by reorganizing the government. He divided the kingdom into 120 provinces, each under a governor.

The satraps, or governors, were divided in to three groups and each group was overseen by and accountable to an official. Daniel was appointed as one of the three officials. He watched their activities and oversaw the financial management of the king's assets and collection of taxes. These three officials held the highest-ranking positions in Babylon and answered directly to King Darius.

Daniel was known to be trustworthy, honest, wise, and righteous of character, while many other officials in the government cheated the king. They stole and hid money,

Darius the Mede

Who exactly was Darius the Mede? In the Book of Daniel, Darius is said to have succeeded to the Babylonian kingdom at the age of sixty-two. But Biblical historians have not been able to find any evidence of this Darius outside of the Bible. What's more, the city and kingdom of Babylon were conquered by Cyrus of Persia, not by the Medes. It has been well-authenticated by historical evidence that Cyrus took control of Babylon and became its king in 539 B.C.E. But there are no records to back up the claim in Daniel that a Median dynasty existed between the Chaldean (Babylonian) and Persian empires.

Some scholars have concluded that Darius is a fictitious literary figure, or a composite figure created by the author of Daniel. Attempts to identify him have resulted in various explanations: he was really Cyrus under a different name. Or, he was Cambyses, the son of Cyrus. Or, he was a special assistant named Gobryas (Gubaru), who took charge of Babylon immediately after Belshazzar, and ruled for about two years, until Cyrus was free to take control. Yet another explanation says he was actually Darius the Great, a real person who ruled the Persian empire from 522 to 486 B.C.E. The debate continues.

Bas relief from a Persian building shows warriors carrying spears and bows.

abused their positions of power, and falsified reports to the king.

Daniel had obtained wealth, power, and position and had done so by only honest means. King Darius knew of Daniel's trustworthiness, and Daniel was soon favored by the new king, who considered elevating Daniel over the other two. When the other officials and satraps learned that the king was thinking of making Daniel the chief authority over all of them, they became jealous and devised a plan to get rid of Daniel.

A TRAP IS SET FOR DANIEL

First the satraps and officials watched Daniel closely, looking for a reason to discredit him. But Daniel was not corrupt, dishonest, or unethical in his duties to the king.

Neither was he negligent. The satraps could not find any justifiable reason to discredit Daniel, so they came up with a different plan.

They said, "We will never find any basis for charges against this man Daniel unless it has something to do with the law of his God" (Daniel 6:5). So the men began to devise a scheme to trap Daniel. They knew that he prayed daily to seek God's guidance for his life. They also knew that Daniel did this by praying alone in his room, three times a day. With this knowledge, the jealous advisors went to the king with their devious plan to discredit Daniel.

"O King Darius, live forever! The royal administrators, prefects, satraps, advisers and governors have all agreed that the king should issue an edict and enforce the decree that anyone who prays to any god or man during the next thirty days, except to you, O king, shall be thrown into the lions' den. Now, O king, issue the decree and put it in writing so that it cannot be altered—in accordance with the laws of the Medes and Persians, which cannot be repealed" (Daniel 6:6–8).

They lied to the king. It had not been all the government officials they named. If it really had been all, then it would have included Daniel, and he would never have agreed to pray to anyone except the Supreme God. But the king was manipulated by the lie and flattered that they all wanted to honor him. So King Darius ordered the decree to be issued.

Anyone who disobeyed the decree would be put to death in the lions' lair. This means of punishment was a common practice under Persian law. The lions' lair or den was actually a pit or cave in the ground with a small opening near the top. The pit could be closed by placing a large stone over the hole.

DANGER FOR DANIEL

When the Hebrew people became captives in Babylon, they could no longer go to the temple of King Solomon to pray and to worship. So while in captivity it became their ritual to pray at an open window facing their homeland and the ruins of Solomon's Temple in Jerusalem. That was the ritual that Daniel followed each day. Alone in his room, kneeling at an open window and facing Jerusalem, Daniel prayed openly and boldly.

The conspirators took this opportunity to betray Daniel. They reported to the king, "Daniel, who is one of the exiles from Judah, pays no attention to you, O king, or to the decree you put in writing. He still prays three times a day" (Daniel 6:13).

This news distressed the king. He favored Daniel, but the king's edict could not be changed. There was no other way except to have Daniel thrown into the pit of the lions. The conspirators continued to goad the king into action. "Remember, O king, that according to the law of the Medes and Persians no decree or edict that the king issues can be changed" (Daniel 6:15).

DANIEL IN THE LIONS' DEN

The king gave the order and Daniel was arrested, and placed into the pit of man-eating lions. A stone was set over the opening of the pit, to make sure that Daniel could not escape and to be sure that no one could rescue him. Then Darius sealed the den shut. The den was sealed by placing wax or clay over the spot where the door opened. While the wax or clay was still soft, the king and his nobles pressed a symbol into the soft material using a signet ring or medallion. The symbol on the ring or medallion identified the sealer. The next day, if the seal was unbroken, the king and all the nobles could then be

This Roman mosaic from the fifth century C.E. depicts Daniel in the lions' den.

certain that no one had tampered with opening the door of the den.

That night the king hardly slept, and at the first sign of daylight, he hurried to the lions' den. In an anguished voice Darius called out to Daniel. "Daniel, servant of the

A 19th-century illustration of Daniel praying in the lions' den.

living God, has your God, whom you serve continually, been able to rescue you from the lions?" (Daniel 6:20).

Daniel respectfully replied, "My God sent his angel and he shut the mouths of the lions. They have not hurt me, because I was found innocent in his sight. Nor have I ever done any wrong before you, O king" (Daniel 6:21, 22).

God's power had saved Daniel. The king was overjoyed to see him and to see that he was not hurt. He had Daniel removed from the pit; now the conspirators faced an angry king. They tried to convince the king that someone must have fed the lions a large amount of meat or that the lions were sick, so that they were not hungry. So Darius ordered a large amount of meat to be fed to the lions. He waited until the lions had eaten their fill. When it was certain that the lions were full, King Darius placed judgment on Daniel's enemies.

Bel and the Dragon

Some stories set during the years of Persian rule over Babylon appear as part of the book of Daniel in the version of the Bible used by Roman Catholics and Eastern Orthodox Christians, but not in the Hebrew Bible or in the Bible used by Protestant churches.

One of these stories involves Bel, another name for Marduk, the chief god of Babylon. According to this tale, each day Babylonian priests gave Bel six barrels of fine flour, forty sheep, and wine. Cyrus asked Daniel why he didn't worship Bel, and Daniel responded that he worshipped only the living God. The king insisted that Bel was a living god, and he set out to prove it. The king told the seventy priests of Bel to set the customary food and wine before the idol. After the priests leave, and with only the king present, Daniel orders ashes to be scattered on the floor of the temple. During the night, the priests, and their wives and children enter the temple through a secret entrance and consume everything. The next morning the king sees the footprints made by the priests of Marduk and their families. Enraged, Cyrus puts them all to death. Then he hands the statue of Bel over to Daniel to destroy.

The second story, of the dragon, is also considered to be deutero-canonical—that is, accepted by some Christians as scripture but rejected by others. Like the story of Bel, the tale of the dragon exposes the Babylonian practice of idol worship as a worthless and vile tradition. When the story begins, the king has ordered Daniel to worship the dragon Bel, in keeping with Babylonian religious custom. But Daniel asks for permission to slay the dragon—without sword or club. He makes cakes out of boiled pitch, fat, and hair. He feeds the cakes to the dragon and it bursts. The Babylonians come enraged, and demand that the king turn him over to them. They also accuse the king of becoming a Jew, which scares the king. Daniel is thrown into a lions' den, but after seven days, he emerges unharmed. The king, upon seeing Daniel, acknowledges the one true God of Israel.

Darius ordered Daniel's accusers and their families to face the punishment they had plotted for Daniel. And the lions, even though full, ate the accused before they reached the floor. This gave even further evidence that it was God who had shut the mouths of the lions.

Darius was now convinced of the power of God, and he wrote a message saying so to all the people in his kingdom:

> May you prosper greatly! I issue a decree that in every part of my kingdom people must fear and reverence the God of Daniel. For he is the living God and he endures forever; his kingdom will not be destroyed, his dominion will never end. He rescues and he saves; he performs signs and wonders in the heavens and on the earth. He has rescued Daniel from the power of the lions (Daniel 7:25–27).

After this incident, Daniel lived peacefully and prosperously under the reign of King Darius and Cyrus the Great. He was held in higher honor than ever before, and he lived out his days writing about the visions and prophesies that God gave him.

PREDICTION AND PROPHECY

The Book of Daniel is like a memoir. The first six chapters are narrated in the third person—the story is about him. But starting with chapter seven, the story is mostly told by him.

It begins in the first year of the reign of King Belshazzar. Daniel was lying in his bed when an unusual dream came to him. In fact, it was so unusual that he wrote it down, because he didn't want to forget it. In the dream he saw "the four winds of heaven," stirring up "the great sea." Suddenly, four beasts emerged from the raging sea, and each beast was different. The first beast was a lion with the wings of an eagle. This lion-eagle stood upon its hind legs, and its wings were plucked off and it was given the mind of a man.

The second beast looked like a ravenous bear, and it had three ribs in its mouth. The third looked like a leopard, except it had four wings and four heads, and this beast was given dominion over a wide area. The fourth beast had teeth that were made of iron and ten horns. This animal was very powerful, and it crushed and devoured its victims and trampled anything under its feet.

Daniel contemplated the meaning of the dream. As he thought about it, yet another vision came into his mind. "While I was thinking about the horns, there before me was another horn, a little one, which came up among them; and three of the first horns were uprooted before it. This horn had eyes like the eyes of a man and a mouth that spoke boastfully" (Daniel 7:8).

DANIEL'S DREAM INTERPRETED

There is a mythological quality to Daniel's dream of the four beasts and little horn. Like so many other aspects of the Book, historians have pored over the meaning of these passages. Many, but not all, agree that the four beasts represented four Godless kingdoms: the Babylonian, the Medo-Persian, the Greek, and the Roman.

Even in the ancient world, the lion was considered the king of the beasts, and at the time of Daniel's captivity, the Babylonian empire was the "king" of the world. And its leader Nebuchadnezzar had his "wings plucked" when he went insane.

The Medo-Persian kingdom was symbolized by the bear. The small Syrian bear was fairly common during that time in history, and it was much less dangerous than the lion. It only attacked when irritated, such as when a female bear senses her cubs are in danger. The third beast, which resembled a leopard, symbolized the Greek Empire, under the rule of Alexander the Great. The leopard is the fastest land animal, and history tells us that Alexander the Great traveled faster and conquered more land than any other man in all recorded history. The fourth, symbolized by a beast with horns, was Rome. The ten horns of Rome are ten kings.

The "little horn" symbolizes the Greek king Antiochus Epiphanes, who tried to destroy Jewish worship and customs. Antiochus IV prevented Jews from celebrating their religious holidays, and he set up an altar honoring pagan gods of foreign countries in King Solomon's Temple. Antiochus IV also tried to force the Jewish people to worship him like a god.

THE ANCIENT OF DAYS AND THE SON OF MAN

In the next part of Daniel's vision, an image of God is revealed. When Daniel described the dream, he referred to the Almighty God as the "Ancient of Days."

> The Ancient of Days took his seat. His clothing was as white as snow; the hair of his head was white like wool. His throne was flaming with fire, and its wheels were all ablaze. A river of fire was flowing, coming out from before him. Thousands upon thousands attended him; ten thousand times ten thousand stood before him. The court was seated, and the books were opened (Daniel 7:9–10).

But the "little horn" was not afraid of the awesome power of God, and continued to be boastful and to speak out against God. Then Daniel saw that the "little horn" was destroyed and thrown into the blazing fire. The other four beasts, the ones that had arisen out of the sea, had lost all of their power also.

Daniel continued to describe the last part of his dream, "In my vision at night I looked, and there before me was one like a son of man, coming with the clouds of heaven. He approached the Ancient of Days and was led into his

In the New Testament, Jesus speaks of the Messiah's coming using language similar to that found in Daniel 7:13. According to the account in the Gospel of Matthew, Jesus tells his followers, "For as lightning that comes from the east is visible even in the west, so will be the coming of the Son of Man. . . . At that time the sign of the Son of Man will appear in the sky, and all the nations of the earth will mourn. They will see the Son of Man coming on the clouds of the sky, with power and great glory. And he will send his angels with a loud trumpet call, and they will gather his elect from the four winds, from one end of the heavens to the other" (Matthew 24:27, 30–31). Statue of Christ the Redeemer in Rio de Janeiro, Brazil.

presence. He was given authority, glory and sovereign power; all peoples, nations and men of every language worshiped him. His dominion is an everlasting dominion that will not pass away, and his kingdom is one that will never be destroyed" (Daniel 7:13–14).

Christians interpret this last vision as symbolizing the coming of the Messiah—Jesus Christ, the king of kings. He comes in clouds to claim his throne, and he is given his eternal throne by his Father, the Ancient of Days.

DANIEL'S VISION OF A RAM AND A GOAT

About two years after the dream of the four beasts, another prophetic dream came to Daniel. In this dream, Daniel saw himself away from Babylon. He was standing in the fortress of Susa, in the providence of Elam, next to the Ulai Canal. In this dream or vision, Daniel again saw strange animals.

The first animal was a ram that stood by the Ulai Canal. The ram had two horns, but they were different lengths, one longer than the other. The ram was a powerful animal. It charged to the west, the north, and the south, and it trampled everything in its path. No other animal was as powerful as the two-horned ram.

As Daniel was thinking about the strange ram, another animal appeared in the vision. The next animal was a goat. This was not an ordinary goat, but a goat with just one horn between his eyes. The goat was swift and powerful, and he moved across the earth without his feet even touching the ground. The goat had a fierce power, and in a rage the goat charged the two-horned ram. The two-horned ram and the one-horned goat battled. When the battle ended, the goat had broken off the ram's horns and trampled the ram into the ground. The goat was too powerful for the ram and there was no one who was able to help or rescue the two-horned ram.

After the goat had defeated the ram, the goat became even more powerful. His appearance changed. He lost the one big horn and in its place grew four new horns. The horns changed again. Out of one of the four horns came a small horn. It began small, but it grew and grew until it reached the heavens.

The horn that grew until it reached the skies attacked what Daniel referred to as the Beautiful Land, which is how Daniel referred to the homeland of the Hebrew people or the country of Israel. The horn that had grown to such a mighty size threw stars down from the heavens and trampled on them. Then this strange life-like horn decided it wanted to rule over creation and called himself the Prince. Finally, the horn would not allow the people to practice their religious ceremonies or to worship God. The horn committed terrible acts against God and God's people. In this part of the dream, the horn seemed to be successful in everything it did.

Daniel noted in his dream that he heard a voice. It was the voice of a holy being. The voice of the holy being asked, "'How long will it take for the vision to be fulfilled'" (Daniel 8:13)?

The voice said to Daniel, "'It will take 2,300 evenings and mornings; then the sanctuary will be reconsecrated'" (Daniel 8:14).

DECODING THE SYMBOL
OF THE RAM AND GOAT

In Daniel's first dream of the four unusual beasts, the symbolism referred to the whole world. In the second dream dealing with the ram and the goat, the symbolism was different, however. It referred specifically to the Hebrew people, their homeland of Israel, Israel's capital of Jerusalem, and their sacred place of worship, Solomon's Temple.

While Daniel tried to understand the meaning of this dream, an angel appeared. Daniel heard a voice from God commanding the angel to explain the dream to Daniel.

A Jewish man holds a Torah scroll at the Western Wall, a retaining wall that is all that remains today of the Jewish Temple in Jerusalem. The Biblical book of Ezra describes how the Persian king Cyrus allowed a community of Jews to return to Israel around 536 B.C.E. and rebuild the Temple. The Temple was ultimately destroyed by a Roman army in 70 C.E.

The Archangel Gabriel makes his first appearance in the book of Daniel. In the New Testament, this messenger from God would announce the births of John the Baptist and Jesus. This gold-painted ikon depicting Gabriel is of Byzantine origin and dates from the 14th century.

The angel's name was Gabriel, which means "man of God" or "God is mighty."

Daniel recognized the awesome power of this heavenly being and immediately knelt in honor. Gabriel explained that he brought a message concerning future events. Daniel was so overwhelmed by the presence of this heavenly being that he fainted. Gabriel touched Daniel, lifted him to his feet, and restored his alertness.

Gabriel explained that the first ram with two horns represented the kings of Persia and Media. They were King Cyrus and King Darius, who together ruled the Persian-Mede Empire. For a time, the Persians and the Medes would be powerful and their conquests would be great.

The next part of the dream, the shaggy goat with one horn, represented the first king of Greece. The large horn that broke off, which was replaced by the four smaller horns, represented the end of the first king. His kingdom would be divided into four smaller kingdoms and would be ruled by four new kings who would not be as powerful.

As for the little extra horn that had grown out of one of the four horns, Gabriel explained that this small horn represented an evil king who had no regard for the One True God. This king would be destructive and persecute the Jewish people, but God had determined an end time for that persecution.

When Gabriel had explained the dream to Daniel, he instructed Daniel to keep the meanings secret because they were about the distant future. Daniel grieved over the future persecution of his people, causing him to become so ill he could not return to his duties at court for several days.

INTO THE FUTURE

Understanding the Book of Daniel, with all of its vivid symbolic imagery, is not a simple matter. Chapter 7, in particular, came seem especially baffling. Jewish and Christian historians and scholars have not come to absolute agreement on what the contents of this chapter mean.

Daniel was so stricken with fear about the vision of the four beasts that he kept it to himself. It was later Christians who assigned meaning to this particular part of the narrative, saying the overall message is that God will emerge victorious, over all nations. People living under oppressive circumstances, especially in countries ruled by dictators and tyrants, must not lose hope: God is ultimately in charge and He will right all wrongs.

Many of the events that Daniel glimpsed in his dreams happened after his death. The ram, for example, symbolized the Persian-Mede Empire. Persia was the stronger of the two countries and was represented by the ram's larger horn. The goat with one large horn was the Greek empire led by Alexander the Great. When the large horn broke off, it symbolized the breakup of Alexander's empire after his death in 323 B.C.E. The four horns that grew next represented the Grecian leaders who replaced Alexander the Great and divided the Greek Empire into four divisions.

The last horn that grew out of the four horns represented Antiochus IV. It is known today that it was 2,300 evenings and mornings from the time that Antiochus invaded the Temple until it was restored by the Jewish people, the time God had determined.

Daniel may not have known the details of his visions as we know them today. But God allowed him to know through his dreams and visions that a better day was ahead for him and his people.

MEDITATIONS AND MESSENGERS

In 538 B.C.E., in first year of King Darius' reign, the Hebrew people had been captives in Babylon for sixty-eight years. Daniel was an elderly man, but he was also wealthy and held in high political esteem, by none other than the king himself. He wore royal robes of the finest materials, lived in a palace, and ate choice foods.

Daniel knew from studying the writings of the prophets that the Hebrew people would be held captive for seventy years. This fact deeply troubled him; he understood that the sinful ways of the Jews had tried God's patience and provoked Him to use the Babylonians to conquer Judah.

In a show of contrition, Daniel took off his royal robes and dressed in sackcloth. While sitting in ashes, he began to pray and fast, confessing his own sins to the Lord, and he prayed of repentance and intercession for the whole Jewish nation.

When Daniel had finished confessing, he asked God for forgiveness and then he asked God to allow the people of Judah to once again live in the land that God had promised to them.

As Daniel prayed an angel named Gabriel appeared. "Daniel I have now come to give you insight and understanding. As soon as you began to pray, an answer was given, which I have come to tell you, for you are highly esteemed" (Daniel 9:23).

DANIEL'S VISION OF A MAN

Sometime between the years of 536–534 B.C.E., God gave Daniel one final vision. He was with a group of compan-

Daniel's Prayer

O Lord, the great and awesome God, who keeps his covenant of love with all who love him and obey his commands, we had sinned and done wrong. We have been wicked and have rebelled; we have turned away from your commands and laws. We have not listened to your servants the prophets, who spoke in your name to our kings, our princes, and our fathers, and to all the people of the land. Lord you are righteous, but this day we are covered with shame . . . because we have sinned against you. The Lord our God is merciful and forgiving . . . Now, our God, hear the prayers and petitions of your servant. For your sake, O Lord, look with favor on your desolate sanctuary. Give ear, O God, and hear; open your eyes and see the desolation of the city that bears your Name. We do not make requests of you because we are righteous, but because of your great mercy. O Lord, listen! O Lord, hear and act! For your sake, O my God, do not delay, because your city and your people bear your Name (Daniel 9:4–19).

Ruins of Persepolis, one of the capitals of the ancient Achaemenid Empire of Persia established by Cyrus the Great. The Achaemenid Empire lasted for more than 200 years, until it was defeated by Greek armies around 330 B.C.E.

ions by the Tigris River. When he looked up, he saw a heavenly being that looked like a man dressed in linen and wearing a gold belt, with a face so bright it looked like lightning.

Only Daniel could see the vision, though the other men felt its presence. Daniel's frightened companions ran away, and hid, leaving their friend alone.

Daniel, too, was afraid, but the messenger of God told him to put aside his fears, explaining that he had come so that Daniel might understand future world events.

WHAT THE MESSENGER REVEALED

The messenger began by revealing the reign of four more kings of Persia. These kings would find themselves engaged in countless struggles, for power, land, and

The Macedonian ruler Alexander (356–323 B.C.E.) was one of the greatest military leaders of all time, conquering territory stretching from Egypt to India. After Alexander's death the vast Hellenistic empire was divided among Alexander's generals. Ptolemy became ruler of Egypt and founder of the Ptolemaic dynasty. Seleucus established a dynasty that would rule the Greek lands until 146 B.C.E. At that time, Rome incorporated the Greek territories into its sphere of influence.

wealth. Year after year, king after king, nations would rise up and then be defeated.

Eventually an evil and untrustworthy leader would rise to power. He would break treaties and invade lands, plunder and loot, distributing the wealth to his own followers as a way to buy their loyalty. The messenger assured Daniel that this evil leader would stay in power only as long as God Almighty decided.

During all of this political upheaval, some of the Hebrews would abandon their faith. Others would stay faithful to God. The messenger explained to Daniel that it would be a difficult time for the faithful people of God. They would be persecuted, their homes would be taken away, they would be exiled, and their very lives would be threatened. But this, too, would only last a period of a time that God had determined.

PROPHECY INTERPRETED

Daniel lived about 2,500 years ago, and some of what the messenger of God explained to him has occurred. The Babylonian Empire (602–539 B.C.E.) was followed by the Achaemenid Persian Empire (539–330 B.C.E.). The messenger said there would be three kings of Persia followed by a fourth one who was the richest and most powerful of them all. This king was King Xerxes, but when he tried to fight against the Grecian army, he left in defeat. This marked the end of the Persian Empire.

The messenger then told of a mighty warrior, now known as Alexander the Great, who was the famous leader of the Greek army. His empire, established around 330 B.C.E., was the one that was divided into four kingdoms to the north, south, east, and west. Today these kingdoms are identified as Greece, Asia Minor, Syria, and Egypt.

Then, the messenger told of the evil leader Antiochus IV, who would rise up and take control of Jerusalem. Antiochus murdered his brother to gain the throne. Known for his deception, lies, and broken treaties, he made it against the law to practice the Jewish religion. Some Jews complied with Antiochus IV in order to escape persecution. During his reign, he "attacked Jerusalem, killed 80,000, took 40,000, and sold 40,000 Jews into slavery. . . . Antiochus again invaded Egypt. But the Roman fleet compelled him to withdraw. . . . He vented his anger against Jerusalem and desecrated the temple."

Antiochus IV continued warring against his neighboring countries until he died of a mysterious disease in 164 B.C.E. By then, the Greek Empire had lost its position as a world power. It was supplanted by the Roman Empire, which would dominate the Middle East for the next several centuries.

ANOTHER UNHOLY KING

The messenger continued to speak to Daniel, and told him of a king who was yet to come. This king would not honor the Almighty God. Instead he would demand the worship of himself, and forbid the worship of anything or anyone else. He would have power and wealth and be known throughout the entire world. Gold, silver, and precious stones would decorate his clothing and his body.

This future king would have many followers, including other world leaders. He would praise and give high honors, power, and wealth to those who follow him. His desire would be to rule over the world's economy, along with a goal to gain absolute control over all the mighty nations of the world.

This would be a time of wars and worldwide destruction. Because the destruction would be so great and

The well-trained armies of the Roman Empire made it the greatest power of the ancient world. Rome gained control of the land of Israel (known at the time as Judea) around 63 B.C.E., and stationed a garrison to impose order on the rebellious Jewish people through force. Jesus was born and conducted his public ministry during the period of Roman rule over Judea, and Roman soldiers carried out his execution on the cross.

include the entire world, this time period is referred to as "end times." But this king's reign would not last forever. The messenger reassured Daniel that it would only continue for as long as the God Almighty had set forth.

THE END TIMES

The messenger whom Daniel said looked like a man (Daniel 10:4) continued with the final portion of his message. He told Daniel that there would be hope for his people, that God would save them, and that He had written their names in the Book of Life. He explained to Daniel that there would be a resurrection, where the dead would be raised to life.

Concluding, the messenger-angel told Daniel not to worry—God would never stop caring for him, even until the end of time. "As for you, go your way till the end," the angel said. "You will rest, and then at the end of the

Angels on High

The ancient Egyptians, Phoenicians, Greeks, and indeed, all nations in history have expressed a belief in angels, according to Wilmington's Guide to the Bible. The Hebrews believed there were four great angels: Gabriel, who reveals the secrets of God to men; Michael, who fights God's foes; Raphael, who receives the departing spirits of the dead; and Uriel, who summons people to judgment.

In the Bible, angels are mentioned in thirty-four books, appearing a total of 273 times. Created by God, angels are invisible and innumerable spirit beings. They are inferior to God, superior to men, and possess personalities. They protect, comfort, minister to believers at the moment of death, and they inform, instruct and interpret the Word of God. There are also different types of angels: archangels (Gabriel is an archangel whose name means "the mighty one of God."), cherubim, seraphim, living creatures, ruling angels, guardian angels, angels associated with horses and chariots, and evil, or fallen, angels.

days you will rise to receive your allotted inheritance" (Daniel 12:13).

NEW BEGINNINGS

Around the year 536 B.C.E., King Cyrus allowed the Hebrew captives to return to Jerusalem. They were allowed to rebuild their temple, and Cyrus arranged for the Hebrews to have gold and silver to help with the rebuilding. The king also returned the holy vessels which King Nebuchadnezzar had stolen some seventy years earlier.

Daniel's prayer had been answered and many of the freed captives returned to the homeland of their ancestors, but many others stayed in Babylon. Daniel was one of those who stayed behind. He had spent almost his entire life in Babylon, and he was now in his nineties.

As God's servant, Daniel had been protected and blessed by God, from the start of his exile to the very end.

FAITH, PRAYER, AND HOPE

Daniel's story is one for all time. It is about the character of God and the character of Daniel—and God is the main character. He is present from start to finish, orchestrating the affairs of men and nations. He raises up world leaders, even ruthless ones, and He brings them down. Wealth, influence, and prosperity flow from Him, and God exacts a price for these gifts: He expects His people to hold themselves to the highest standard of moral and ethical conduct, no matter what hardships come. The character of Daniel exemplifies the type of behavior God expects of His own.

On the surface, some might say that the Book of Daniel is a memoir, about a Jewish teen that is taken hostage when his country is invaded, and he ends up spending the rest of his life in a foreign land. He manages to rise to positions of power, wealth, and influence because God endows him with a special gift to understand the meanings of dreams and vision.

But there are so many invaluable lessons to be learned from him in this Biblical narrative. For example, Daniel shows us how to stand up for what we believe in. He believed in one Supreme God, one Creator, and he was willing to die to preserve his faith in God. He also teaches us that God is the source of all life and all meaning in life. Daniel depended on God to show him the way, in all circumstances. For this, God richly rewarded him.

Daniel further serves as an example of someone who obediently and consistently followed the will of God. In the world today it is easy to do good, when the people who mean the most to us are present, watching over us, keeping us in line. But what happens when we're on our own: do we stray? Do we follow the crowd? Do we do what's most convenient at the time? Do we laugh at jokes that poke fun at other people, even when we know we shouldn't? Do we tell little white lies, or run a red light when no one is looking? Daniel lived a life of moral excellence, and the decision to live an uncompromising life came not from his parents, or rabbi, or even his three co-captives. It came from him.

Daniel also shared his faith with idol-worshipping kings, the very kings who sought to kill him on more than one occasion. "The Book of Daniel is a textbook for cross-cultural ministry whenever a believer finds himself in the midst of a hostile environment towards God and His followers," author Les Brittingham writes. "This is where the primary focus of interpretation and application of the Book of Daniel should be placed."

Brittingham further states that "Daniel . . . is a book about lifestyle. This great prophet assures us of God's sovereignty in the affairs of men and encourages us to demonstrate a lifestyle of commitment to the living God, regardless of the relentless force of opposition."

Finally, Daniel's confession of sin, followed by an earnest request to God for mercy and forgiveness for the Hebrew people, has been recognized by many Biblical commentators as an outstanding example of prayer. And perhaps this is Daniel's greatest gift to generations today. Though features of the Book of Daniel remain in dispute—the authorship, the prophecies, the dates and names of key events and figures—its main themes of faith, prayer, and hope have withstood the test of time.

Notes

CHAPTER ONE: HOPE FOR HIS PEOPLE

page 16:   "In terms of its impact . . ." David Van Bierna, et al., "The Twenty-five Most Influential Evangelicals in America," *Time*, February 7, 2005.

page 17:   "The Book of Daniel . . ." Les Brittingham, *Decoding Daniel: An In-depth Study of the Book of Daniel* (Longwood, Fla.: Xulon Press, 2007).

CHAPTER THREE: LIFE IN BABYLON

page 30:   "for when Babylon . . ." Marc Van de Mieroop, *The Ancient Mesopotamian City* (New York: Oxford University Press, 1999), p. 95.

page 30: "Mesopotamia was . . ." Stephen Bertman, *Handbook to Life in Ancient Mesopotamia* (New York: Oxford University Press, 2003), p. 210.

page 32:   "There was a tower of solid . . ." Bertman, *Handbook to Life in Ancient Mesopotamia*, p. 196.

page 34:   "Mesopotamia is the birthplace . . . " Sigfried Giedion, *The Eternal Present: a Contribution on Constancy and Change* (New York: Pantheon Books, 1964), p. 21.

CHAPTER FIVE: FACING THE FIERY FURNACE

page 53:   "Many people worship luck . . ." Wayne Edward Oates, *Luck, A Secular Faith* (Louisville, Ky.: Westminster John Knox Press, 1995), pp. xi–xii.

CHAPTER SEVEN: THE LAST BANQUET OF BABYLON

page 63: "In 1853 an inscription . . ." Henry H. Halley, *Halley's Bible Handbook with the New International Version*, 25th Edition. (Grand Rapids, Michigan: Zondervan Publishing House, 2000) p. 435.

page 69: "Archaeologists have excavated . . ." Beth Moore, *Daniel: Lives of Integrity, Words of Prophecy*. (Nashville, Tennessee: LifeWay Press, 2006), p. 94.

CHAPTER TEN: MEDITATIONS AND MESSENGERS

page 94: "attacked Jerusalem . . ." Halley, *Halley's Bible Handbook with the New International Version*, p. 444.

page 98: "The Book of Daniel . . ." Brittingham, *Decoding Daniel*, p. xxii.

page 98: "Daniel . . . is a book about . . ." Brittingham, *Decoding Daniel*, p. xiv.

Glossary

Ark of the Covenant—a chest in which the Jewish people kept the Ten Commandments, along with other cherished items of the Jewish faith.

concubine (noun)—a woman that lives with a man without being his wife.

contrite (adjective)—penitent; contrition (noun): remorse, regret, sorrow.

cuneiform writing—composed of strokes having the form of a wedge or arrowhead.

consecrate (verb)—to make or declare holy.

demoralize (verb)—to corrupt in morals; to weaken in discipline or spirit; to erode or destroy the courage, confidence or hope of a person or group.

dominion (noun)—supreme authority.

eunuch (noun)—A castrated man in charge of a harem.

incarnate (adjective)—embodied in flesh; given a bodily, especially a human, form.

indoctrinate (verb)—to systematically and thoroughly teach somebody a belief, doctrine, or ideology.

intercession (noun)—prayer or petition in favor of another

pinnacle (noun)—the highest point.

prophet (noun)—a person who communicates God's word or who speaks through divine inspiration; prophecy (noun): the function or vocation of a prophet; a declaration of something to come.

repent (verb)—to turn from sin and resolve to reform one's life.

sovereign (noun)—one possessing the supreme power and authority in a state.

vassal (noun)—a person, nation, or group that is dependent on, subordinate to, or under the protection of another.

ziggurat (noun)—an ancient Mesopotamian pyramid-shaped tower, rising in stories of ever-decreasing size, with a terrace at each story and a temple at the top.

Further Reading

BOOKS FOR YOUNG READERS

Kee, Howard Clark, ed. *The Learning Bible*, Contemporary English Version. New York: American Bible Society, 1995.

Kimmel, Eric A. *Wonders and Miracles, A Passover Companion.* New York, New York: Scholastic Press, 2004.

Student Bible, Contemporary English Version. Grand Rapids, Mich.: Zondervan Publishing House, 1996.

Teen Study Bible, New International Version. Grand Rapids, Mich.: Zondervan Publishing House, 1998.

Wilkinson, Philip. *Eyewitness Christianity*. New York: DK Publishing, Inc., 2006.

BOOKS FOR ADULTS

Bertman, Stephen. *Handbook to Life in Ancient Mesopotamia*. New York: Oxford University Press, 2003.

Brittingham, Les. *Decoding Daniel: An In-depth Study of the Book of Daniel*. Longwood, Fla.: Xulon Press, 2007

Coogan, Michael D., and Bruce M. Metzger, eds. *The Oxford Companion to the Bible*. New York: Oxford University Press, 1993.

Flavius, Josephus. *Josephus, The Essential Writings*. Edited by Paul L. Maer. Grand Rapids, Mich.: Kregel Publications, 1988.

Frick, Frank S. *A Journey Through the Hebrew Scriptures*. Belmont, Calif.: Thomson/Wadsworth, 2003.

Halley, Henry H. *Halley's Bible Handbook with the New International Version*. Grand Rapids, Mich.: Zondervan Publishing House, 2000.

Hill, Jonathan. *Handbook to the History of Christianity*. Grand Rapids, Mich.: Zondervan Publishing House, 2006.

Oates, Edward Wayne. *Luck, a Secular Faith*. Louisville, Ky.: Westminster John Knox Press, 1995.

Practical Christian Foundation. *Daniel, In God I Trust*. Holiday, Fla.: Green Key Books, 2004.

Internet Resources

http://www.Bible-history.com

> This Web site is a basic Bible encyclopedia. It offers excellent graphics, maps, pictures and time lines. It is easy to simply type in your subject and find related materials.

http://www.Biblical-art.com

> Art and paintings that pertain to Biblical art are featured on this site.

http://www.Jewishencyclopedia.com

> This encyclopedia-style Web site is specific to the Jewish religion. It offers information on the historic Hebrew Bible and also modern day information of Jewish holidays and rituals.

http://Jewishvirtuallibrary.org

> Jewish history, news, and publications come to life on this site, which allows you to take a virtual "trip" to Israel.

http://MyJewishlearning.com/history

> Designed like a newspaper, this Web site begins with Jewish history and continues to guided learning on issues related to modern Judaism.

Index

Numbers in **bold italics** refer to captions.

Illustration Credits

CHERYL PADEN grew up in rural Nebraska and attended a one-room country school. She graduated from college and worked for fifteen years as a registered nurse. Desiring to devote more time to writing, Paden retired from nursing.

From a young age, Paden enjoyed the Bible stories she learned in Sunday school, and never gave up her desire to study the Bible. Paden works part-time as a local pastor and continues her education at the Saint Paul School of Theology in Kansas City, Kansas. Combining both her love for writing and Bible study, Paden has worked as a freelance writer, publishing inspirational stories and non-fiction articles for the past ten years. Paden, her husband and three sons live in Fremont, Nebraska.